Market Tantrums and Monetary Policy

Proceedings of
the U.S. Monetary Policy Forum 2014

CHICAGO BOOTH

Initiative on
Global Markets

Published, sold and distributed by:
now Publishers Inc.
PO Box 1024
Hanover, MA 02339
United States
Tel. +1-781-985-4510
www.nowpublishers.com
sales@nowpublishers.com

Outside North America:
now Publishers Inc.
PO Box 179
2600 AD Delft
The Netherlands
Tel. +31-6-51115274

ISBN (print): 978-1-68083-486-4
E-ISBN (epub): 978-1-68083-487-1
E-ISBN (pdf): 978-1-68083-503-8

Table of Contents

Foreword

The U.S. Monetary Policy Forum (USMPF) is an annual conference that brings academics, market economists, and policymakers together to discuss U.S. monetary policy. A standing group of academic and private sector economists (the USMPF panelists) has rotating responsibility for producing a report on a critical medium-term issue confronting the Federal Open Market Committee (FOMC).

The 2014 USMPF panel includes private-sector members Michael Feroli (JP Morgan Chase), David Greenlaw (Morgan Stanley), Jan Hatzius (Goldman Sachs), Ethan Harris (Bank of America Merrill Lynch), Peter Hooper (Deutsche Bank), as well as academic panelists Stephen Cecchetti (Brandeis), James Hamilton (UC San Diego), Anil Kashyap (Chicago Booth), Frederic Mishkin (Columbia), Hyun Song Shin (Princeton), Kermit Schoenholtz (New York University) and Kenneth West (Wisconsin).

This volume reports the results of the eighth USMPF conference, held on February 28, 2014 in New York, N.Y.

The eighth USMPF report, "Market Tantrums and Monetary Policy," authored by Feroli, Kashyap, Schoenholtz, and Shin, reports on interactions between monetary policy and financial stability. Following the authors' presentation, Narayana Kocherlakota, President of the Federal Reserve Bank of Minneapolis and Jeremy Stein, Board of Governors of the Federal Reserve System, offered their comments.

This year's policy panel was entitled "Lessons for Communications Policy from Our Experiences with Unconventional Monetary Policy" and was moderated by Martin Wolf, chief economics commentator, *Financial Times*. The discussion featured presentations by Charles Evans, President of the Federal Reserve Bank of Chicago, Charles Plosser, President of the Federal Reserve Bank of Philadelphia, and Sayuri Shirai, Member of the Policy Board of the Bank of Japan.

The USMPF is sponsored by the Initiative on Global Markets at the University of Chicago Booth School of Business.

ANIL K KASHYAP AND FREDERIC S. MISHKIN, CO-DIRECTORS
CHICAGO, ILLINOIS, AND NEW YORK, NEW YORK, MAY 2018.

U.S. Monetary Policy Forum 2014 Report

Market Tantrums and Monetary Policy

*Michael Feroli, Anil K Kashyap, Kermit Schoenholtz,
and Hyun Song Shin*

ABSTRACT

Assessments of the risks to financial stability often focus on the degree of leverage in the system. In this report, however, we question whether subdued leverage of financial intermediaries is sufficient grounds to rule out stability concerns. In particular, we highlight unlevered investors as the locus of potential financial instability and consider the monetary policy implications.

Our focus is on market "tantrums" (such as that seen during the summer of 2013) in which risk premiums inherent in market interest rates fluctuate widely. Large jumps in risk premiums may arise if non-bank market participants are motivated, in part, by their relative performance ranking. Redemptions by ultimate investors strengthen such a channel. We sketch an example and examine three empirical implications. First, as a product of the performance race, flows into an investment opportunity drive up asset prices so that there is momentum in returns. Second, the model predicts that return chasing can reverse sharply. And third, changes in the stance of monetary policy can trigger heavy fund inflows and outflows.

Using inflows and outflows for different types of open-end mutual funds, we find some support for the proposition that market tantrums can arise without any leverage or actions taken by leveraged intermediaries. We also uncover connections between the destabilizing flows and shocks to monetary policy.

We draw five principal conclusions from our analysis. First, in contrast with the common presumption, the absence of leverage may not be sufficient to ensure that monetary policy can disregard concerns for financial stability. Second, the usual macroprudential toolkit does not address instability driven by non-leveraged investors. Third, forward guidance encourages risk taking that may subsequently reverse. In fact, our example suggests that when investors infer that monetary policy will tighten, the instability seen in summer of 2013 could reappear. Fourth, financial instability need not be associated with the insolvency of financial institutions. Fifth, the tradeoffs for monetary policy are more difficult than is sometimes portrayed. The tradeoff is not the contemporaneous one between more versus less policy stimulus today, but is better understood as an intertemporal tradeoff between more stimulus today at the expense of a potentially more challenging and disruptive policy exit in the future.

Of course, our analysis neither invalidates nor validates the policy course the Federal Reserve has actually taken. Any such conclusion depends on an assessment of the balance of risks given the particular circumstances. This lies beyond the scope of our paper. Instead, our paper is intended as a contribution to developing the analytical framework for making policy judgments. But our analysis does suggest that unconventional monetary policies (including QE and forward guidance) can build future hazards by encouraging certain types of risk-taking that are not easily reversed in a controlled manner.

"Participants also reviewed indicators of financial vulnerabilities that could pose risks to financial stability and the broader economy. These indicators generally suggested that such risks were moderate, in part because of the reduction in leverage and maturity transformation that has occurred in the financial sector since the onset of the financial crisis."

FEDERAL OPEN MARKET COMMITTEE MINUTES, DECEMBER 2013

Introduction

The quote shown above has become almost boilerplate language that appears in various Federal Reserve speeches and testimony. It is usually closely followed by saying that monetary policy is not the first line of defense against financial vulnerability. Instead, monetary policy should focus primarily on inflation, employment and growth, while micro- and macroprudential tools should be used to deal with sources of financial instability. This doctrine is sometimes called the *separation principle* of policy design.

We understand well the implications of leverage for financial stability. Indeed, the 2008 USMPF report was one of the first to highlight the potentially severe consequences of the looming subprime mortgage crisis (Greenlaw, Hatzius, Kashyap, and Shin (2008)). In this report, however, we question whether subdued leverage of the banking sector is sufficient grounds for monetary policy to disregard financial developments.

Our focus is on market "tantrums" such as that seen during the summer of 2013 in which risk premiums inherent in market interest rates fluctuate widely. We highlight the potential for non-bank market participants to drive such events and consider the implications for monetary policy. Because fluctuations in the risk premium have consequences for real economic decisions such as consumption and investment, market tantrums deserve attention from policy makers. That said, the implications for monetary policy will clearly depend on how much lasting impact market tantrums have on real economic decisions, a subject that we do not address in this paper.

We sketch an example in which large jumps in risk premiums arise due to the actions of non-bank market participants who are motivated, in part, by their relative ranking in comparison to others. As we make clear, this example is *not* the only channel through which large fluctuations in risk premiums may arise. When other non-bank channels of financial instability are present, these channels may amplify the market impact if they operate in concert. We then examine the empirical evidence to help us assess whether non-bank channels of financial instability can be inferred from the data. This study does not distinguish between the possible non-bank channels for market disruption, but instead looks only for evidence of their potential existence.

To anticipate our conclusions, we find some empirical backing for the proposition that *financial market disruptions can arise without any leverage* or actions taken by leveraged intermediaries. Our evidence comes from fixed income mutual fund flows and their interactions with price changes, in which we find mutually amplifying impact of price changes and flows. We also uncover connections between the destabilizing flows and shocks to monetary policy.

Less clear is whether such destabilizing effects are large enough and persistent enough to warrant policy makers to reassess in a fundamental way the tradeoff between stimulating real activity and financial stability. Further research is needed in this area.

On the other hand, because the usual regulatory tools designed to deal with leveraged intermediaries cannot address the financial instability caused by non-bank market participants, the burden of proof for whether such effects deserve due consideration by policy makers is less onerous.[1] In other words, whereas the instability generated by excessive leverage can be addressed (at least in part) by strengthened banking regulation, the instability generated by non-banks has no simple remedy. For this reason, the market tantrums we analyze may deserve attention from monetary policy makers even if their economic impact is smaller than the impact of banking sector distress.

The idea presented in our example is that delegated investors such as fund managers are concerned with their relative performance compared to their peers, an idea familiar from earlier works, such as Rajan (2005) and Borio and Zhu (2012). One reason for this concern regarding relative performance may be that it affects their asset gathering capabilities. We explore a mild version of the concern for relative performance – a type of "friction" absent in textbook macro models. In particular, we suppose that investing agents are averse to being the last one into a trade. Although this feature may sound innocuous, it can potentially set off a race among

---

1.   Tucker (2014) highlights the contrast between the progress made in the regulation of banks versus non-banks.

investors to join a sell-off in a race to avoid being left behind. The analogy is with a game of musical chairs. During a boom, the same incentives push investors into chasing yield. The yield-chasing behavior in our model comes about through delegated decision-making, but other behavioral assumptions can generate similar investor dynamics.[2]

The effects examined in our paper would be even more potent if redemptions by claimholders on investment vehicles generate run-like incentives. Chen, Goldstein and Jiang (2010) provide evidence that redemptions from mutual funds holding illiquid assets create incentives like those facing depositors in a bank run, as in Diamond and Dybvig (1983). Money market funds (MMFs) may face an acute form of vulnerability to runs, as argued by the Squam Lake Group.[3]

Our example points to three implications that we explore empirically. First, as a product of the race, flows into an investment opportunity drive up asset prices so that there is momentum in returns. Second, the model predicts that return chasing can reverse sharply. And, third, changes in the stance of monetary policy can trigger heavy fund inflows and outflows.

We provide evidence to support these model implications. Our first piece of empirical analysis shows that the kind of return-chasing behavior presumed by the model is present for certain types of fixed income mutual fund flows. Specifically, we verify that when asset flows for certain fixed income securities are high, prices persistently rise and that a feedback loop emerges. High flows lead to rising prices, which attract more flows, which further raise prices. An important caveat is that this pattern is absent for US Treasuries and not statistically significant for equity markets, where prices seem to equilibrate quickly.

The co-movement of fund flows across several asset classes provides evidence for the second model implication: the sharp reversal of return chasing. Informally, we show that in certain time periods large flows in the same direction occur for selected types of funds. These bullish and bearish dates line up with anecdotal descriptions of bond market sentiment. More formally, we examine the characteristics of the first principal component of the fund flows, representing the common factor in fund flows. This common factor is constructed so as to explain the maximum variance of the series being considered. We call this factor an index of bond market sentiment because it exhibits many abrupt changes and the timing of these changes often coincides with the dates identified by the informal analysis. These periods also sometimes coincide with large price movements.

---

2.   For instance, Becker and Ivashina (2013) document reaching for yield on the part of insurance companies in their investments in corporate bonds.

3.   Squam Lake Group (2011) "Reforming Money Market Funds" http://www.squamlakegroup.org/Squam%20 Lake%20MMF%20January%2014%20Final.pdf

Third, we show that monetary policy surprises are a statistically important determinant of fund flows and that flow adjustments induced by policy are associated with significant price effects. Because monetary policy is a coordinating factor for funding costs, changes in beliefs about the current stance of monetary policy or updates about the future path of policy can be a powerful force that influences investors and fund managers. We confirm this prediction by showing how bond market sentiment and behavior relate to monetary conditions.

We draw five principal conclusions from our analysis. First, in contrast with the common presumption, the absence of leverage may not be sufficient to ensure that monetary policy can disregard concerns for financial stability. To be sure, excessive leverage was implicated in the recent crisis (Greenlaw et al, 2008). However, it does not follow that future bouts of financial instability will operate only through the same mechanism that was present in 2008 and 2009.

Second, the strongest version of the separation principle is incorrect. Taming bond market flows cannot easily be accomplished via the usual list of macroprudential tools such as bank capital ratios, bank liquidity requirements, haircut regulation on repurchase agreements, or loan to value ratios. Conversely, the stance of monetary policy directly contributes to some of these flows. Our results complement the evidence that an important channel of monetary policy runs through the fluctuations in risk premiums. Shiller, Campbell and Schoenholtz (1983) provided early evidence on how market prices "overreact" to monetary shocks. Hanson and Stein (2012) and Gertler and Karadi (2015) add to the accumulated evidence.

Third, forward guidance has the potential to be a particularly powerful factor in influencing the forces identified in our model. The events of the summer of 2013 have been called an anomaly by many observers. The benign interpretation is that risks had been mispriced and that, over the course of the summer and fall, communication by the Federal Reserve has helped correct that problem. Under this view, the error has been eliminated and the lack of disruption to markets with the onset of tapering in December confirms that risks have been contained.

But the interpretation from our model is more nuanced. The Fed may have succeeded in 2013 in convincing market participants that slowing the pace of bond purchases is a separate decision from decisions about the path of future interest rates. Hence a shift in risk appetite that was beginning in the summer of 2013 has been deferred. However, this issue could reappear when policy accommodation is finally removed.

Indeed, our reading of the Fed's actions once balance sheet shrinkage began in 2017 is that the central bank paid considerable attention to this possibility. Fed policymakers went to great lengths to signal that although the balance sheet would decline, there would not be outright asset sales and that the path of interest rates would not move in lock step with the balance sheet changes. Consequently, a change in one instrument may signal very little about the other. Perhaps as a result, overall financial conditions remained loose well after interest rates had risen above zero.

The financial market turbulence in early 2014 associated with emerging market (EM) assets and currencies appears consistent with our analysis, and with the scenarios laid out in Shin (2013) and Turner (2014). Selling pressure was evident in EM mutual funds, with fund managers citing a flight by retail investors that triggered the largest outflows in several years.[4] This development seemed to catch many by surprise even though the U.S. Treasury's Office of Financial Research (OFR) had highlighted just such a risk in their 2013 *Annual Report* published a month earlier. Specifically, the OFR (2013) indicated that: "Yield-seeking capital flows across borders, driven by both external and domestic factors, have driven a decline in local [EM] bond yields. Markets for emerging-market bonds have grown increasingly more sensitive to changes in U.S. interest rates." Clearly, deterioration in the growth prospects of significant EM economies could have a meaningful impact on the global economy.

Moreover, the bout of EM turbulence in early 2014 shows that periods of instability might wind up being blamed on Fed policy decisions irrespective of whether such disruptions are directly attributable to Fed actions. Market jitters followed several weeks after the December 2013 FOMC meeting and there had been no new information regarding the Fed's policy path since that time. In addition, there is some evidence that emerging market investors were discriminating on the basis of fundamentals.[5] Still, press reports have tied the late-January 2014 sell-off in risk markets to Fed policy actions.[6]

Fourth, financial instability need not be associated with the insolvency of financial institutions. To be sure, asset managers, fund managers and other delegated agents with little effective leverage do not become insolvent in the way that banks or highly leveraged hedge funds do. Nor, for that matter, would other yield-chasing, long-only agents investing on their own behalf. Consequently, the fallout from an investor-driven bout of instability is not likely to be of the same magnitude as the collapse of a credit bubble.

----

4.   In fact, accounts of this episode differ. "'Retail investors are running for the exits. They see the turmoil, they read the newspapers and they have a shorter time horizon,' said Michael Ganske, head of Emerging Markets at Rogge Capital Partners, a fixed income fund with $59 billion under management." Source: David Oakley et al. *Financial Times*, "Investors pull $12 billion from EM stock funds," January 31, 2014. In contrast, Bloomberg cites subsequent data suggesting that retail investors did not panic and were buying on net. See Ben Steverman, "Pros Panic, Retail Investors Stay Cool on Emerging Markets," February 13, 2014. http://www.bloomberg.com/news/2014-02-13/pros-panic-while-retail-investors-stay-cool.html

5.   See Kristin J. Forbes, "Don't Rush to Blame the Fed," *The New York Times*, February 5, 2014.

6.   For one example, see http://online.wsj.com/news/articles/SB10001424052702303448204579340480156732234?-mod=ITP_pageone_0.

Nevertheless, the lack of leverage does not rule out a meaningful impact on the real economy through financial instability. When bond yields soar, lending rates to households and firms will also be affected. These shocks could have a direct impact on GDP growth through subdued investment and consumption. Stein (2014) provides some evidence that is consistent with possibility.

While the purpose of tightening monetary policy is to slow the pace of economic activity, the type of instability generated by our model can lead to a nonlinear reaction in risk premium, making a "soft landing" more difficult to achieve. Thus, the potentially excessive real economy impact is genuine, even though no institutions fail, and no financial institutions are bailed out using public funds. Unleveraged investors are not "too-big-to-fail" (TBTF) and may not even face a risk of failure. However, focusing exclusively on TBTF would be missing an important channel of the transmission of monetary policy and an important potential source of instability. Vayanos and Woolley (2013) have shown how momentum and reversals result from small agency frictions, even with long-only investors. Our results highlight the need to understand better the market-wide impact of traditional delegated investors.

Finally, our results suggest that the tradeoffs for monetary policy are more difficult than is sometimes portrayed. Even if the real economic consequences of market tantrums are smaller than those that arise from banking sector problems, market tantrums driven by non-banks cannot be addressed by the usual micro- and macro-prudential policies. The absence of an alternative tool for addressing the problems tilts the burden of proof toward those who argue that market tantrums should not be factored into monetary policy considerations.

Having said all this, our analysis neither invalidates nor validates the course the Federal Reserve has actually taken. Any such conclusion depends on an assessment of the balance of risks given the particular circumstances. Such an assessment lies beyond the scope of our paper. Instead, our paper is intended as a contribution to developing the analytical framework for making policy judgments. But our analysis does suggest that the unconventional monetary policies (including QE and forward guidance) create hazards by encouraging certain types of risk-taking that can reverse at some point. These threats are not easily controlled with other tools.

The tradeoff is not the contemporaneous one between more versus less policy stimulus today, but is better understood as an intertemporal tradeoff between more stimulus today at the expense of a more challenging and disruptive policy exit in the future.[7] Acknowledging this tradeoff does not prejudge what the stance of monetary policy should be today. However, it would be important to recognize that there is a genuine tradeoff: stimulus now is not a free lunch, and it comes with a potential

---

7.   See Kocherlakota (2013) for a similar diagnosis of the tradeoff.

for macroeconomic disruptions when the policy is lifted. Consistent with these concerns, the Fed did not take for granted that the domestic macroeconomic fall-out from exit would be as gentle as was the impact from the 2013 "taper tantrum." Instead, well after it began to raise interest rates, and even after it began to shrink its balance sheet, the central bank maintained an accommodative policy stance that was reinforced with strong forward guidance about the path of interest rates. The European Central Bank and Bank of Japan have also been extremely gradual with their balance sheet policies.

The remainder of the report comes in four parts. We first introduce the model that helps shape our thinking about the connections between monetary policy settings and the actions of delegated agents. The key departure from conventional models is the concern of the investors with their relative performance. We show that the model makes three testable predictions about the nature of fund flows and prices.

Next, we describe the data that goes into the construction of the bond sentiment index. The data are taken from Lipper and cover all mutual funds in the United States for six asset classes. We explain some of the measurement challenges involved in working with these data and describe some of their basic properties.

The following section of the paper presents our tests of the model predictions. We first establish that the feedback loop implied by the model is present for four types of fixed income investments. We then use those asset classes to construct our bond sentiment indicator and show that it exhibits some of the reversals that the model predicts. We then show that the sentiment index and the common factor in bond returns are sensitive to monetary policy surprises.

The concluding part of the report identifies some open questions that are raised by our analysis.

1. Unleveraged Investors and Financial Conditions

Contemporary discussions of financial instability are heavily conditioned by the experience of the 2008 crisis, and understandably so. The dangers of excessive lever-age and maturity mismatch were severely underappreciated before the crisis, so they have naturally taken center stage in the policy discussions since. Moreover, policy makers have now elevated leverage to being the touchstone of policies toward financial stability.

However, the "taper tantrum" in the summer of 2013 and its impact on financial markets (especially in the emerging economies) have shown that subdued leverage is not a sufficient condition for financial tranquility.

The "taper tantrum" played out mainly in the fixed income markets, and the protagonists were neither banks nor leveraged nonbank intermediaries. Instead, the protagonists appeared to be "buy side" investors with little effective leverage. Figure 1.1 reports data from Morningstar on fund flows from 2008 up until just before the tantrum and shows how disproportionate the skew toward the fixed income category had been.

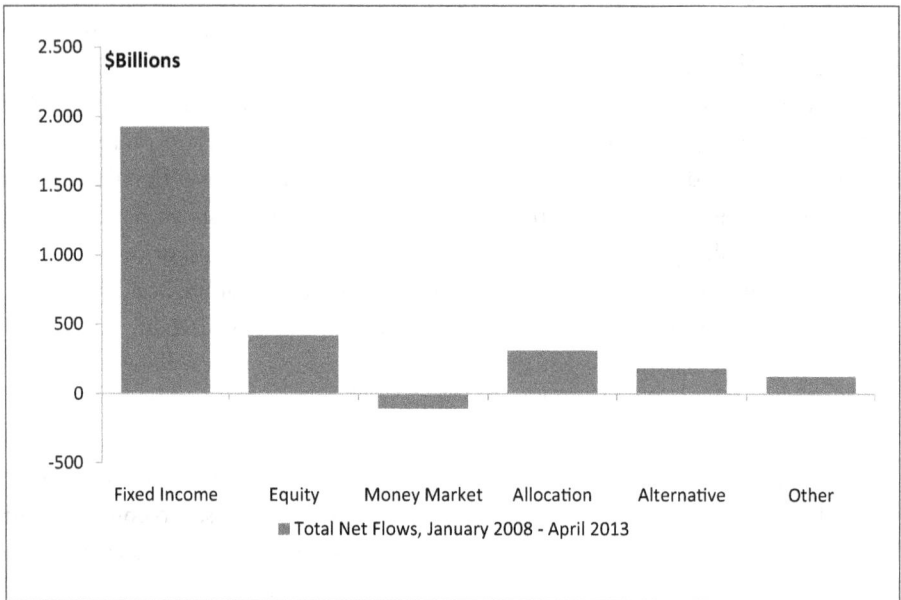

Figure 1.1. Net Worldwide Fund Flows by asset category
(Source: Morningstar)

Textbook buy-side investors are assumed to stabilize markets, as they step in to buy when the price falls and to sell when prices rise excessively, thereby cushioning shocks to financial markets. Instead, as we will see, there is evidence that buy-side investor flows may amplify shocks in fixed income funds rather than dampen them. The evidence is that investors partially sell when the prices fall. Also, sales tend to elicit further price declines, so that price changes and sale volumes may lead to feedback loops that mimic the amplifying distress dynamics more familiar with banks. The January 2014 experience of EM bond funds provides a good example.

One way to approach the issue would be to recognize that the distinction between leveraged institutions and buy-side investors matters less if they share a similar tendency toward procyclicality. Asset managers are answerable to the trustees of the fund that have given them their mandate, while the trustees are themselves agents vis-à-vis their ultimate beneficiaries. As a result, asset managers lie at the end of a chain of principal-agent relationships where contracts will be in place to mitigate the agency problems all along the chain. Often, such contracts will place limits on discretion further down the chain.[8]

To be sure, the typical large asset manager only plays a passive role, fulfilling the wishes of the trustees of the pension fund or sovereign wealth fund that have given the asset manager its mandate. Nevertheless, the investment management contract will reflect agency problems all along the fund management delegation chain. So, irrespective of the origins of the agency frictions, the actions of the asset manager may display procyclicality. For the economy, this outcome can be consequential.

Given the potential for procyclical actions, and the sheer amount of money managed by delegated agents, the usual indicators of vulnerability that were designed and back-tested for past crises (mainly bank-driven events), would not be adequate going forward. In particular, the crisis indicators that were developed by reference to the 2008 financial crisis may be of limited use if the instability is driven by unleveraged buy-side investors. For instance, it would be easy for some policy makers to be lulled into a false sense of security by seeing that banking sector leverage is lower now than it was before the Lehman bankruptcy.

1.1 A Model of Investor Behavior

In this section, we sketch a model of buy-side investors as the locus of financial market volatility. Suppose there are two types of investors. There are *passive* investors—called "households"—who are risk-averse. They choose between holding a risky security (corporate bonds, mortgage-backed securities, long-dated treasuries and so on) or depositing their money in a money market fund (MMF) that earns a floating rate closely tied to the central bank policy rate. The safer choice is to earn the floating rate.

The second group of investors consists of *active* investors, whom we refer to as "delegated agents" (or just agents). These agents are risk-neutral and care about long-term fundamental asset values. However, their behavior reflects an element of short-termism because the agent whose performance is ranked low relative to the others on any particular date suffers a penalty. We could interpret this penalty as the loss of a customer mandate, consistent with the empirical evidence on the relationship between fund flows and fund performance (Chevalier and Ellison (1999)). Thus, the "friction" in the model is that relative performance matters for delegated agents, because relative performance will be the key determinant of fund inflows.

---

8.   See Stein (2013) for other perverse incentives that are created by these kinds of delegated arrangements that can also lead to potential financial stability challenges.

Although delegated agents are risk-neutral and care about the fundamental values of the assets, the element of relative ranking injects spillover effects. Because being ranked low is costly, each delegated agent tries to avoid underperformance relative to the group. However, the more *others* try to avoid underperforming, the harder any particular delegated agent must try to avoid the fate of underperforming.

For simplicity, we do not consider the strains on the delegated manager from redemption pressures. Incorporating such pressures would squeeze the delegated manager from both sides of the balance sheet – namely, price falls on the asset side and redemptions on the liabilities side – making the potential price spirals sketched below even more potent. See Chen, Goldstein and Jiang (2010) for evidence of excessive liquidations arising from redemption pressures in the mutual fund industry.

We do not suggest that our model is the only (or even necessarily the most important) non-bank channel for market tantrums. Other mechanisms that build on redemption pressures generated by myopic investors could cause the same amplifying interactions that we find in our empirical investigation. One possibility is the embedded leverage in investor positions resulting from hedging strategies that replicate put options. We do not take a stand on which mechanisms are most important – any answer to this question needs further study. However, to the extent that the alternative channels are compatible with the mechanism sketched below, they may strengthen the severity of market tantrums.

With those qualifications, imagine a game of musical chairs, where one of the players will end up without a seat. Knowing that being left on the sidelines is costly, all players will scramble to get a seat. However, the harder others try to find a seat, the more effort each must also expend in finding a seat. In this way, the concern of delegated agents about the impact of relative rankings on their payoff injects an element of coordination in their portfolio choice that has the outward appearance of herding behavior. When other delegated agents are selling, the price of the risky security falls, as the sale must be absorbed by risk-averse household investors. Even though the delegated agent cares about the long-term fundamental value, the small element of short-termism that comes from the aversion to underperformance (being left without a chair in the game of musical chairs) may be enough to induce concerted selling by all agents. To solve for when the short-term incentives outweigh the long-term fundamental value, we sketch a simplified version of the global game model of monetary policy developed in Morris and Shin (2014).

Concretely, assume that there are three delegated agents, each with funds sufficient to hold 1 unit of the risky security. They choose between holding the risky security and putting their money in a floating rate money market account. The total supply of the risky security is given by S. All investors care about the fundamental value of the asset at some terminal date T. The expected fundamental value of the risky security is V. Suppose that the households have quadratic utility, and hence the aggregate demand curve submitted by the household sector is linear.[9]

The price of the risky security is determined by market clearing as shown in Figure 1.2. The demand curve for the risky security submitted by the household sector is linear with intercept at V. The delegated agents have demand curves that are horizontal at V up to the limit implied by their total assets under management (AUM). Since there are three agents each with one unit of AUM, the sector demand curve is horizontal up to 3 and then falls off vertically as depicted in Figure 1.2. The slope k of the linear demand curve depends on the risk-aversion coefficient of the household investors, the riskiness of the risky security, and the size of the household sector.

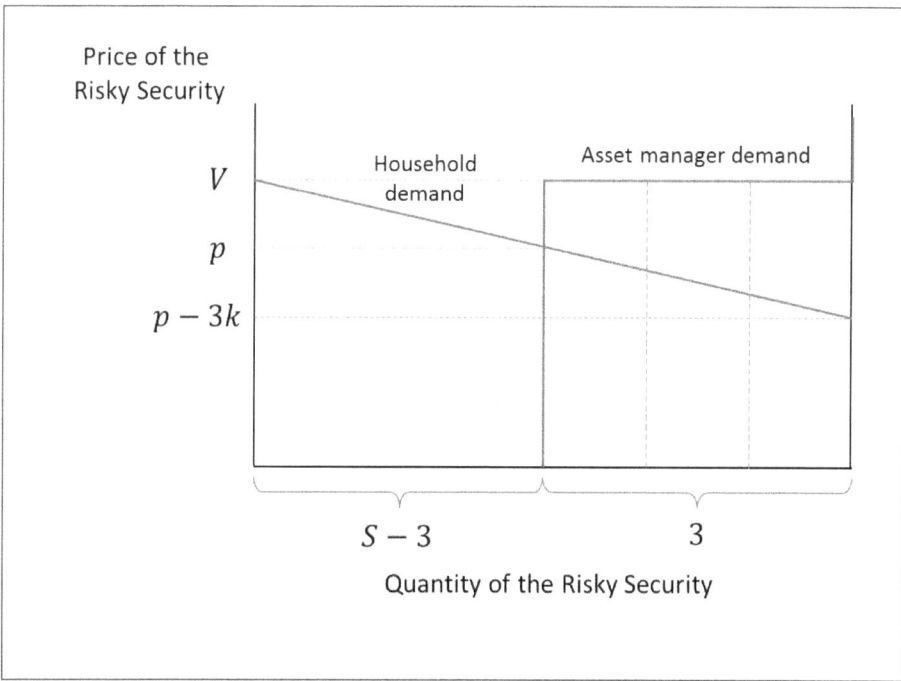

Figure 1.2. Equilibrium in the market for the risky security

The equilibrium price of the risky security is determined by market clearing, and is denoted by p. The market-clearing price is determined so that both households and delegated agents have identical valuations and their total demand equates to the supply

---

9.   The linear demand curve comes from the quadratic objective function $U = Vy - \frac{1}{2\tau}y^2\sigma^2 + (e - py)$ where y is the holding of the risky security, τ is risk tolerance, σ^2 is the variance of risky security payoff and is e investor wealth. The first order condition gives $p = V - \frac{\sigma^2}{\tau}y$, which is linear in y.

of the asset. The expected return to holding the risky security is given by R, defined as the capital gain implied by the terminal price relative to the acquisition price:

$$R = \frac{V - p}{p}$$

The return to leaving money in the floating rate MMF and rolling the position over is given by the product of short-term interest rates. Assume that the central bank is highly transparent, so that the path of future short rates (i_{t+1} and so on) is known with a high degree of certainty. While investors have differences in their signals on the future stance of monetary policy, these differences are small enough that each investor behaves as if the investor exactly knows the future path of the interest rate.[10] Then, the return to the strategy of rolling over the MMF holding is given by r, defined as:

$$r = (1 + i_{t+1})(1 + i_{t+2}) \cdots (1 + i_T) - 1$$

In this context, we interpret forward guidance as a commitment by the central bank to keep short-term rates low for a long period, thereby lowering r, and making the risky security relatively more attractive to hold.

The payoff to holding the risky security depends on how many others are selling it. Table 1.1 gives the payoffs to holding the risky security when the difference in returns $R - r$ between the risky security and the rolling-over strategy is so large that a delegated investor prefers to hold the risky security regardless of what other investors do.

	0 sells	1 sells	2 sell
Risky asset price	p	$p - k$	$p - 2k$
Expected return from risky bond	R	R	R
Expected return from rolling over short bond	r	r	r

Table 1.1. Payoff to holding risky security when holding risky security dominates

In contrast, Table 1.2 depicts the payoffs to holding the risky strategy when concerted selling by the other two asset managers is enough to reduce the interim price low enough so that holding the risky security results in the asset manager

---

10. Technically, investors all receive noisy private signals of the true path of interest rates, but we take the limit as the noise goes to zero.

coming last in the ranking of short-term performance. In Table 1.2, if the other two asset managers sell, then the price of the risky security is driven low so that on a marked-to-market basis the holder of the risky security is ranked last and suffers the penalty C.

While delegated agents are confident about the path of future short-term interest rates, they in fact are receiving slightly noisy signals about it. The global game solves for the threshold level of the interest rate r^* such that a delegated investor holds the risky security when $r \leq r^*$ but switches into the floating rate MMF when $r > r^*$.

	0 sells	1 sells	2 sell
Risky asset price	p	$p - k$	$p - 2k$
Expected return from risky bond	R	R	$R - C$
Expected return from rolling over short bond	r	r	r

Table 1.2. Payoff to holding risky security when others
selling triggers penalty C

At the switching point in the global game, the uncertainty over the actions of the other delegated agents is given by the uniform density, so that each column of Table 1.2 has probability exactly 1/3. This feature, dubbed the "Laplacian beliefs" of the players, is a general feature of beliefs at the switching point in global games.[11]

Given Laplacian beliefs of uniform density over the number of other delegated agents selling the risky security, the expected payoffs can be obtained from Table 1.2 by weighting each cell of the matrix by 1/3 and adding up. The expected return to holding the risky security is

$$\frac{1}{3} \cdot R + \frac{1}{3} \cdot R + \frac{1}{3}(R - C) = R - \frac{1}{3}C$$

The return to holding the short-term instrument is r. Therefore, the delegated agent prefers to hold the risky security provided that

$$r \leq R - \frac{1}{3}C = \frac{V - p}{p} - \frac{1}{3}C$$

From this, we can solve for the threshold value of the price where all delegated agents switch from the risky security to the short-term instrument. Delegated agents hold the risky security as long as price is lower than a threshold:

---

11.   Morris and Shin (2014) give a formal treatment of this issue.

$$p \leq \frac{3V}{C + 3(1 + r)}$$

From this basic result, we can build up the following features of the model.

As long as $p \leq 3V/(C+3(1+r))$, any new delegated investor that enters the market will buy the risky security. When the size of the household sector stays constant, the new purchases of the risky security shift the holdings from the household sector to the asset management sector, so that the price is bid up. As the delegated management sector's holdings cumulate, the price will approach the upper bound from below.

The central bank can raise the upper bound by committing to a path of low short-term rates and thereby lowering r. This action will induce more agents to buy the asset and will push up its price. This mechanism is the "risk-taking channel" of monetary policy.

However, in this model, there is an asymmetry in the operation of the risk-taking channel. The central bank can encourage the accumulation of risk positions by committing to lower rates, but the unwinding of those positions cannot be done smoothly. When the central bank changes course, and signals that future rates will have to rise, doing so will raise r. If the increase in r is big enough so that $p > 3V/(C+3(1+r))$, then the trigger point in the delegated agents' strategy is breached and all of them sell the risky asset. This leads to a collapse in the price of the risky security from p to $p - 3k$.

Because the delegated investors are risk-neutral, the returns to holding the risky asset can be interpreted as the risk premium. The risk premium before the price collapse is

$$R = \frac{V - p}{p}$$

The risk premium following the price collapse is

$$R' = \frac{V - p + 3k}{p - 3k} > \frac{V - p}{p}$$

The longer the forward guidance is in place, the larger will be the positions of the delegated agents relative to the household sector. Consequently, the price reversal following a long period of expansionary monetary policy will be much larger than the price reversal following a short period of expansionary monetary policy.

One important determinant of the size of the amplification of shocks is the size of the delegated management sector. From Figure 1.2, we see that the market-clearing price rises (leading to compressed risk premiums) as the size of the delegated management sector becomes large relative to the total stock of the risky security.

However, the larger is the delegated management sector, the more potent is the impact of the "musical chairs game", and the bigger is the price impact of concerted sales. If, in addition to their ranking, the delegated agents care about the *extent* of the price declines, then the incentives to avoid a bottom ranking become even sharper. Given the potentially greater impact of the whiplash effect, the critical threshold interest rate r^* in the global game switching strategy is lower when the delegated management sector is larger. Indeed, the global game places an upper bound on the size of the delegated management sector that is consistent with low risk premiums.

Figure 1.3 illustrates the impact of the growth of the delegated management sector. On the one hand, the risk premium becomes compressed initially as more assets are controlled by the delegated management sector. However, as the sector grows, the regime becomes more fragile as the trigger for the switching point falls. The central bank is increasingly driven into the corner – quite

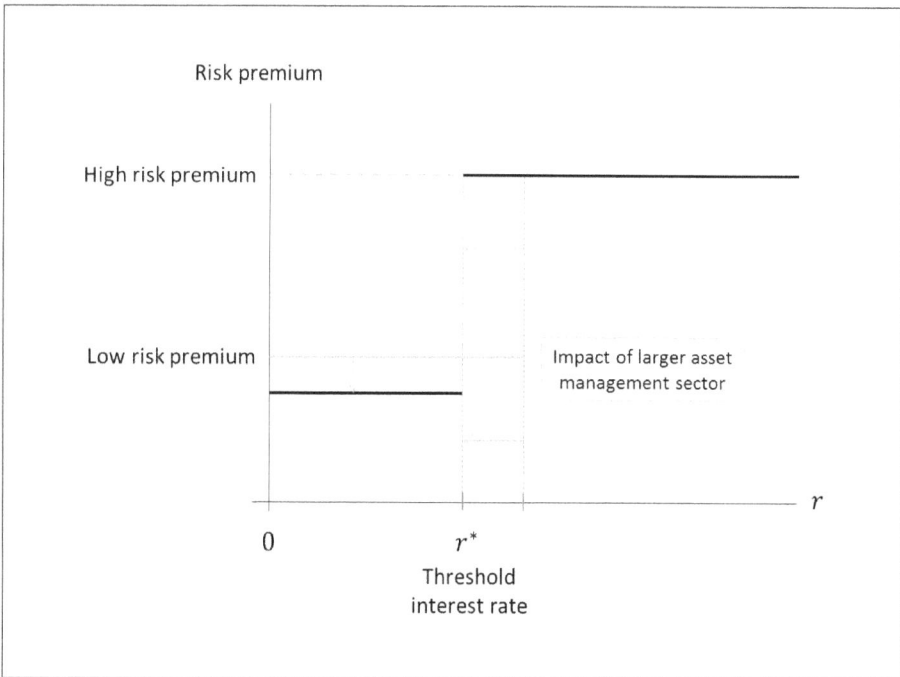

Figure 1.3. Impact of the growth of the asset management sector
(adapted from Morris and Shin (2014)

literally – as shown in Figure 1.3, as it takes ever-stronger beliefs about the low level of returns associated with the safe investment strategy to support the low risk premium regime.

The dynamic in Figure 1.3 suggests that forward guidance will have the desired effect of lowering risk premiums and raising asset prices. However, one unintended side effect of this strategy is to increase the potential for a larger snapback in the yields once the perceived yield on riskless assets begins to rise.

Indeed, with market entry of delegated agents (or growing holdings by the existing managers), the size of the delegated management sector will increase up to the limit that is consistent with the low risk premium regime. When the economy finds itself in such circumstances, even a very small prospective increase in the risk-free interest rate will be sufficient to trigger the jump in the yield of the risky security. In this simple version of the model, reassurances from policymakers that the eventual rise in rates will be gradual and managed carefully cannot prevent the sharp jump in yields. That jump is the consequence of a much more basic friction – that of aversion to underperformance on the part of the fund managers and the musical chairs game that it engenders.

In this simple example, the longer the expansive monetary policy is in place, the larger the eventual market shock. In a more complex version of the model, the greater issuance activity of the borrowers spurred by a low risk premium can magnify the effects sketched above. In this context, central bank asset purchases reduce the amount of risky securities held by the public, but when monetary tightening coincides with the end of central bank asset purchases, the resulting market shock will be that much larger.

Figure 1.4 shows the typical time path of delegated agent holdings and the risk premium following the triggering of the jump of yield. Delegated agent holdings initially decline sharply due to the "musical chairs" game. While subsequent high-risk premiums draw them back into the market, the tighter monetary environment implies that the size of asset management sector holdings consistent with the low risk premium regime is smaller after the shock. So, the upper panel of Figure 1.4 shows a partial recovery in delegated agent holdings, but not enough to restore the level that prevailed prior to the monetary tightening.

The implications for market risk premia are shown in the lower panel of Figure 1.4. The risk premium starts at very low levels, but jumps after the monetary tightening shock. The risk premium subsequently subsides, but not to its previously low level. In this sense, monetary policy shocks have persistent effects.

One important lesson from this brief theoretical excursion is that *quantities matter*. In this respect, the lesson is similar to the one from the banking crisis of 2008. Just as we would be concerned with a rapid increase in bank balance sheets and

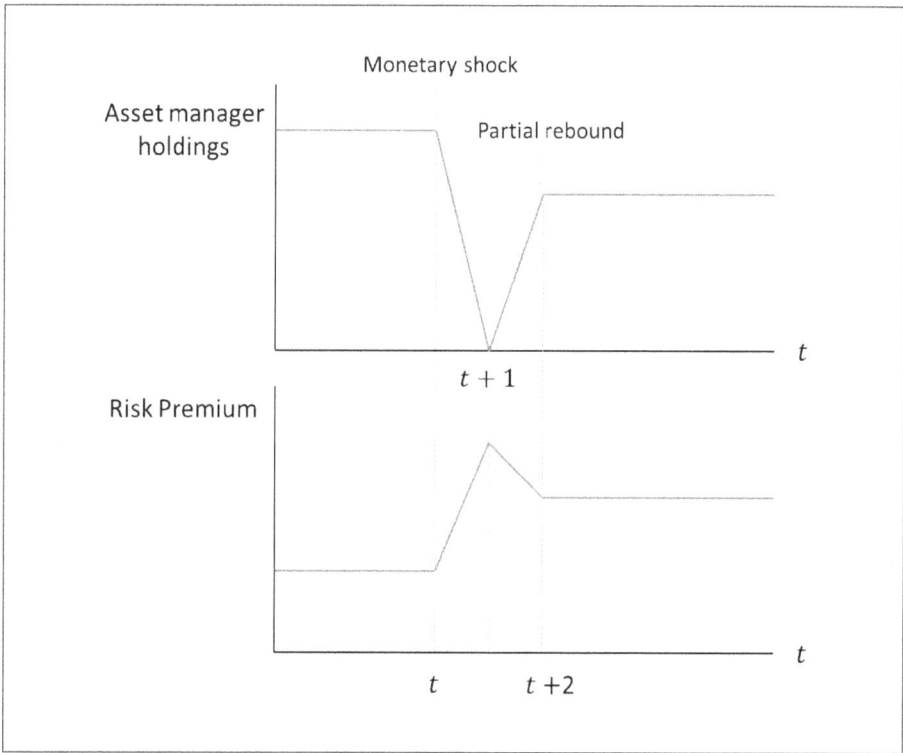

Figure 1.4. Time paths for delegated agent positions and risk premiums
following monetary tightening

credit, we should similarly be interested in the size of the holdings of fixed income securities of buy-side investors, provided that these investors have the potential for procyclical actions. In the example sketched above, the size of the asset holdings of the delegated management sector plays the role of a state variable that determines both the risk premium in boom times *and* the trigger point from the low-risk premium regime to the high-risk premium regime.

2. Data Description

The primary data that we analyze are flows into and out of mutual funds and the associated changes in market values of assets under management. Assembled by Lipper, a firm that specializes in supplying mutual fund information, the data are intended to be a snapshot of the fund industry at a given point in time. We begin by describing measurement issues before presenting the basic characteristics of the data.

2.1 Measurement Issues in Mutual Fund Flows

Lipper collects the data in two ways. Some mutual funds report data *each week* while others report *monthly*.

Weekly data are collected as of Wednesday (except on holidays when the data are collected on a Tuesday). Weekly-reporting funds provide both the asset values in week t and the change in the value of the assets from week t-1. In principle, the following identity should hold:

$$\text{Assets}_{t+1} = \text{Fund flows}_t + \text{Change in Market Value of Assets}_t + \text{Assets}_t \quad (1)$$

Lipper uses (1) to deduce flows. There are, however, four qualifications to bear in mind: a firm can merge with another one, a fund can be liquidated or created, a fund can change its principal investing area, or a fund might not report at all. In any of these cases, the end-of-period assets and beginning-of-period assets are inconsistent, leading to a mistaken imputation of the flows. Unfortunately, these events happen periodically and can lead to end-of-period asset values that are too high (which can happen in a merger) or too low (when a liquidation occurs).

Monthly-reporting firms provide retrospective information for the prior month (without any weekly breakdown). For example, in early February, these firms would report their assets as of the beginning and end of January, along with the market performance during January. The funds that report on a monthly basis tend to be larger than the weekly reporters. A similar recursion to (1) should also hold at the monthly level as well, but the same reporting problems also can occur for the monthly reporting funds.

These problems have two implications for our work. First, and most importantly, a complete analysis of the flows and returns requires working at the monthly frequency. As we explain below, we will test one aspect of the model using the weekly data, but a complete description of the data can only be done by aggregating to the monthly frequency. Accordingly, most of the empirical work relies on monthly data.

Second, every means of correcting the reporting problems is unavoidably imperfect. We opt to use the noisy imputed flows from Lipper to form a revised series for assets that respects (1). While this undoubtedly creates measurement error in each of the individual series, these errors seem to wash out when we look for common patterns across different asset classes. For example, we recorded all the instances when (1) failed to hold in the originally reported data from Lipper. While there are many cases where the identity fails, the deviations do not seem to cluster around key periods that we highlight in the subsequent analysis. Hence, we believe that measurement problems are not responsible for the principal conclusions that we draw about the co-movements in these series.

2.2 Mutual Funds Flows and Valuation Changes

We use Lipper data on six different categories of mutual funds. These are: U.S. Treasury Securities (UST), High Yield U.S. Corporate Bonds (HY), Investment Grade U.S. Corporate Bonds (IG), Mortgage Backed Securities (MBS), Emerging Market Debt Funds (EM), and U.S Equities (EQ). Lipper claims to cover 100% of all U.S.-based mutual funds, with roughly 75% of the funds (which represent about 55% of assets) reporting weekly and the remaining funds reporting monthly. The data start in 1992 (for all of the categories except the emerging market series) and end in October 2013. The EM monthly data first become available in October of 1993 but the EM series is implausibly volatile until 1995, so we begin using the data in 1995.[12]

The raw monthly flows are tabulated in three panels of Figure 2.1. We draw three conclusions from the figure. First, the scales on the charts show important differences. The equity market funds are much larger than all the others, and the EM funds are vastly smaller. Second, the flows for all the categories grow over time, as mutual funds in general become more popular investment vehicles. But, the lift-off points for when the flows reached their current levels differ. Finally, and most importantly, all the fixed income flows show occasions when there were abrupt outflows. The equity flows show more overall volatility, but even that series displays many notable sudden outflows.

The associated assets under management for the various categories are shown in Figure 2.2. These charts make the different sizes of the categories much easier to see. Beyond that difference, there are two other points worth noting. First, the evolution of these funds differs. For example, the MBS funds show much less growth than the others. For this category, assets under management in early 2009 were below the level of 1992. The MBS funds undoubtedly were partly affected by the appetite for securities on the part of the government-sponsored enterprises. Second, the outflows during the 2013 taper tantrum were so large and widespread that they affected all of the fixed income funds.

Because of the differences in the growth of the assets over time, it is more informative to look at the flows in comparison to assets, rather than the unadjusted flows. These data are graphed in Figure 2.3. The main problem with this normalization is that some of the biggest moves may be caused by the measurement error described earlier. The reporting problems mean that not all of the large swings shown in this figure are necessarily genuine. But the graph does help show that, relative to assets, there are many cycles that appear common to

---

12.   We could not find anything in the documentation that explains the extreme volatility, but it is very obvious when simply plotting the data.

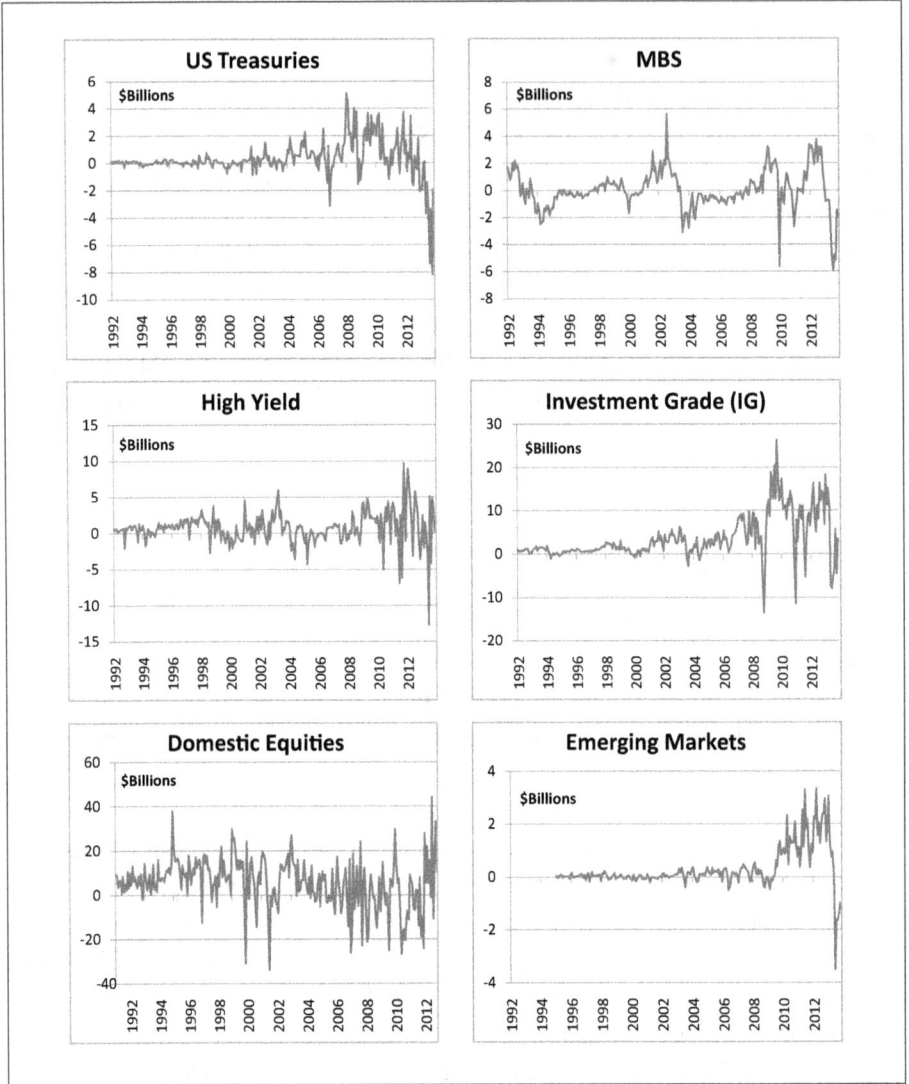

Figure 2.1. Monthly Mutual Fund Flows

the different types of assets and, as mentioned, we do not believe the common movements are due to measurement error. We will use these series in some of the econometric work below.

To display some of the key patterns more clearly, we made two further transformations that are intended to reduce some of the noise. First, we switched from using the asset values that satisfy equation (1) to using the fitted asset values from a regression of the logarithm of assets on a constant and a cubic function of time. This filter eliminates the potentially exaggerated jumps in asset values that can

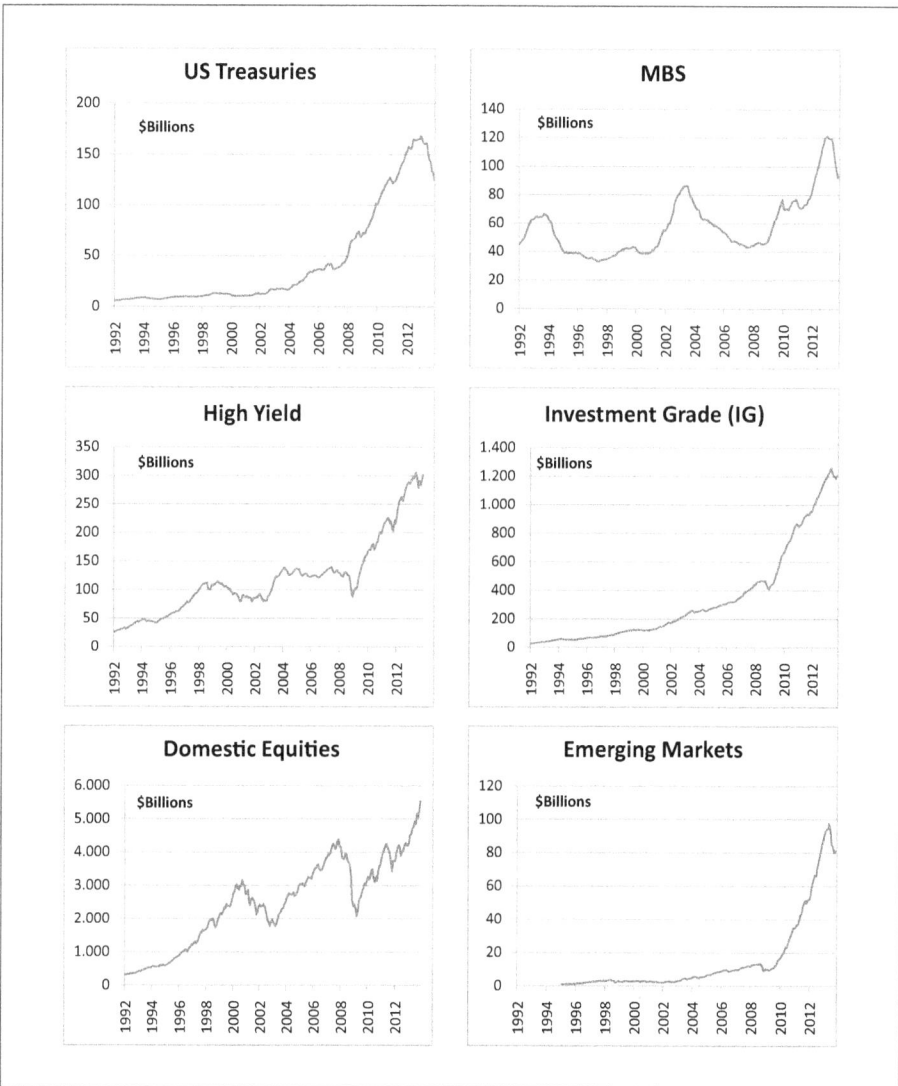

Figure 2.2. Imputed Assets-Under-Management in Different Asset Classes

come from the misreporting. The second change is to replace the raw flows with a weighted average of the flows over the current and previous two months; we used weights of 0.6 on the current month, 0.3 on the prior month, and 0.1 on the flows from two months earlier.[13] This modification also reduces some of the spikes that might come from reporting errors (especially ones that are reversed).

13.   We experimented with other weighting schemes and they did not make much difference provided that they gave substantial weights to prior months.

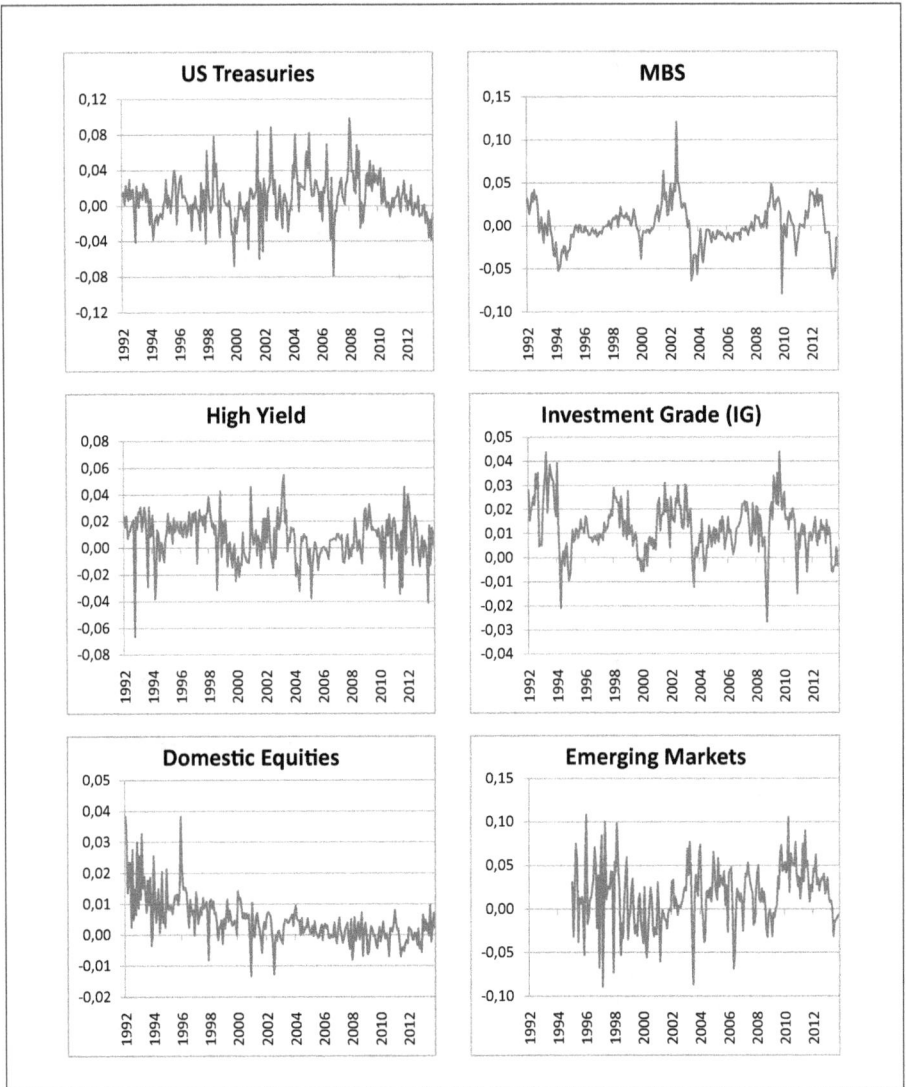

Figure 2.3. Flows Normalized by Imputed Assets Under Management

In addition, the weighting is consistent with the spirit of the model, which suggests that funds that are moved into a position late would be more prone to reverse.

These transformations reveal several interesting features of the data and provide a simple motivation for the more sophisticated econometric analysis that follows. Because we will not use these transformed series in our main empirical work, we did not fine tune the weights. We merely note three intriguing aspects of the patterns that emerge in Figure 2.4.

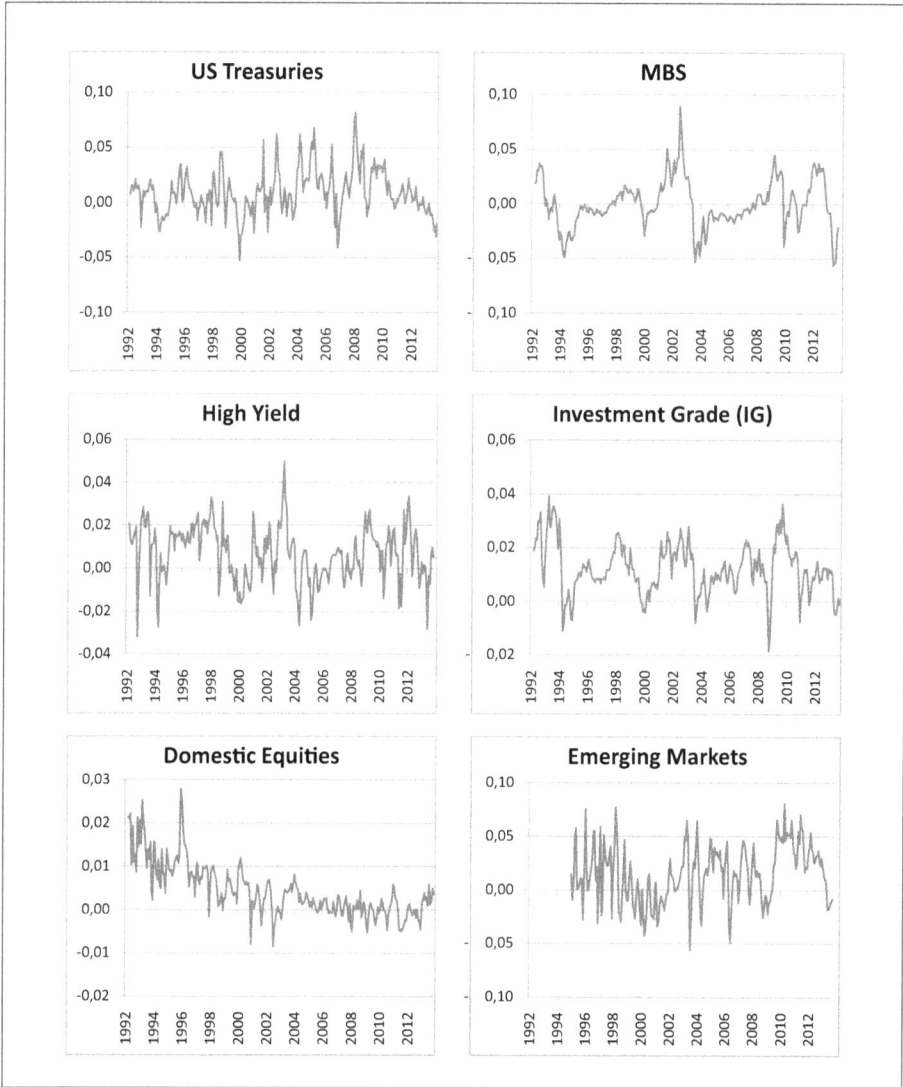

Figure 2.4. Weighted Fund Flows Normalized by Detrended Assets

First, one can see that the patterns for normalized equity flows are quite different than all the others. The flows are smaller, less volatile and bounced around zero for most of the last decade. Our subsequent econometric work will also show that equity funds differ from fixed income funds.

Second, the HY, IG, MBS and EM series share several similar waves. All of them exhibit outflows in 1994 and around the turn of the century. The taper tantrum is another period of synchronized outflows, while in 2003 there is a period of harmonized inflows. These coordinated oscillations will be the focus of most of the econometric analysis that follows.

Interestingly, the Asian financial crisis of the late 1990s played out differently for the various asset classes. While EM funds exhibited outflows, IG and HY funds show inflows.

Third, the Treasury flows are less clearly correlated with the other fixed income flows. In some cases, such as 1994 and 2013, the flows are in a similar direction. But in other cases, such as the 2003 episode, UST flows are in the opposite direction. This difference is not completely surprising because UST flows sometimes reflect a flight to safety, such as in the summer of 1998 at the start of the Asian crisis.

Finally, Figure 2.5 shows the change in market values normalized by assets (at the beginning of the month). These are akin to returns for the different asset classes (subject to the measurement issues described earlier). There are three main observations that we take from Figure 2.5. First, and not surprisingly, the returns are much choppier than the flows. Second, the volatility of returns differs greatly across categories. Naturally, equity returns exhibit much more variation than fixed income returns. But, even within the fixed income categories there are substantial differences. MBS and IG returns are never more than four percent up or down in a month, while EM and HY returns are sometimes much larger (in absolute value) than that. Finally, with the naked eye, it is hard to detect much synchronization across the categories, with the exception of fall 2008, when all the series except MBS show the return for October 2008 to be negative.

3. Assessing the Predictions of the Model

We now examine evidence regarding the main predictions of our model. The first prediction relates to the positive feedback between fund flows and returns. The second regards the synchronization of flows across asset categories. The third explores the connections between monetary policy and fund flows and prices.

3.1 Feedback Loops Between Prices and Quantities

The model introduced in Section 1 implies the existence of "risk-on, risk-off" type switches in bond market sentiment. Accompanying such abrupt changes in sentiment is a feedback loop between fund flows and prices: large fund inflows (outflows) are serially correlated and associated with reinforcing price dynamics. Put

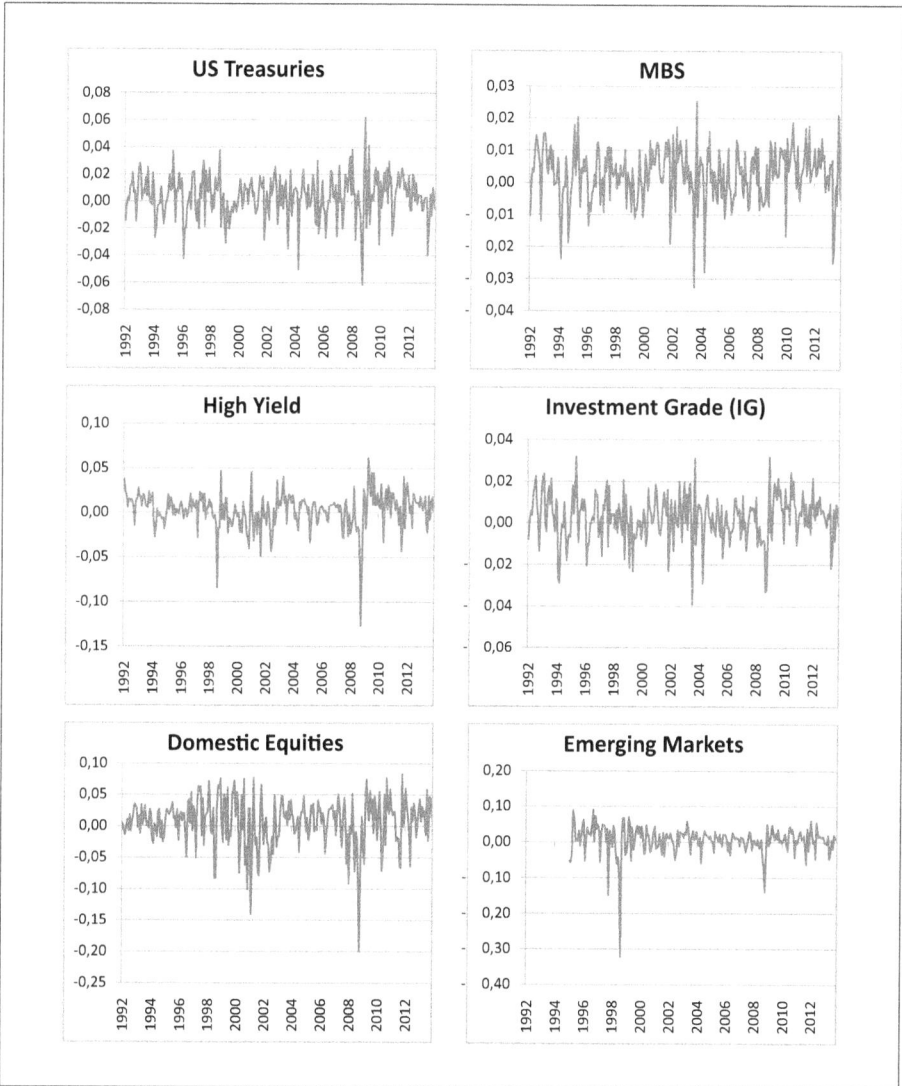

Figure 2.5. Change in Market Values Normalized by Imputed Assets Under Management

differently, fund inflows boost prices that attract (rather than diminish) further inflows, eventually inviting a sharp reversal at a threshold level. In effect, investors' demand for funds becomes upward, rather than downward, sloping over a key interval. Other models may have a similar implication. In what follows, we look for the yield-chasing behavior without distinguishing between alternative mechanisms that might generate it.

To explore this first implication empirically, we examine a set of bivariate vector autoregressions (VARs) that relate fund flows and fund returns for the six mutual fund types defined in Section 2 of the report using the weekly reporting funds only. Each VAR includes four weekly lags of the flows and returns as well as the two-year accumulation of past fund inflows normalized by the asset level prior to that accumulation. This normalized measure serves as a control indicator that proxies for sustained fund accumulation, a key risk factor for flow reversals in the model. In each category, the flows, returns and accumulated flows are scaled by the beginning of period assets.[14] We restrict the analysis to weekly funds because of the identification issues discussed below.

In the body of the report, we focus on the main findings from these VARs. The specific regression coefficients and other summary statistics can be found in the Appendix. The three primary messages that we take from the VARs are:

- As others who study mutual fund flows have found (Chevalier and Ellison (1999)), flows respond positively to fund returns over at least part of the projection interval (with the exception of U.S. Treasuries in our results).
- Returns also respond positively to flows for five of the six fund classes, but not for U.S. Treasuries and not with statistical significance over the full projection interval for equities and high-yield bonds.
- The flow/return responses typically occur soon after the innovation, resulting in cumulative responses that appear substantial over time.

These findings indicate that the feedback loop implied by the model is at least partially present. Moreover, several factors may account for the lack of an observed feedback effect in U.S. Treasuries and the absence of a statistically significant effect over the full projection interval in equities. First, our sample of fund flows covers only part of the universe and may overlook interactions at frequencies higher than weekly. Second, these two markets are relatively deep and liquid, making them less likely to face sudden reversals by investors who rush to sell illiquid instruments first (much as depositors run on a bank). Third, in the case of Treasuries, other powerful considerations – such as flight to quality – may conceal the feedback effect implied by the model.

Turning to the specific results, we present impulse responses based on a Cholesky ordering of each VAR that places fund flows first and returns second. This ordering reflects the model design, in which the destabilizing dynamics are driven by the flows that result from the decisions of investors or of their portfolio managers. The assumption behind this ordering is that shocks to flows in a given week are exoge-

---

14.   In some periods, the weekly data exhibit temporary, discrete jumps that appear to be artifacts of the fund reporting mechanism. We ran the VARs using this raw data and again replacing the raw data with filtered series that substitute for each jump the average of the pre- and post-jump observations. The findings we emphasize are evident in both specifications. We present results using the filtered data.

nous to changes in valuations in that week. After the initial week, however, the VAR allows for arbitrary correlations between the innovations to flows and returns.[15]

We use weekly data in this exercise because we believe that the alternative of using the more comprehensive monthly data would strain the credibility of the causal hypothesis that we are trying to assess. More specifically, over the course of the month, there are likely to be some fundamental shocks that could lead to both higher inflows and higher returns. So using a Cholesky ordering to identify a feedback loop between flows and returns for monthly data would not be convincing.

Ideally, we would have liked to use even higher frequency data (such as daily observations) to test for the feedback loop. At the daily frequency, it would be even easier to defend the assumption that flow movements cause price adjustments. However, daily data are not available. Moreover, even if they were available, we would have to estimate a number of coefficients to assess the long-term magnitude of the effects. As it stands, we assume that within a week the responses are similar across each day of the week. Because the shortest flow frequency that most investors can even observe is weekly, this assumption seems plausible. As supporting evidence, we note that the regression estimates show that much of the price responses to flows occur over a period that is *longer* than one week.

For each of the six fund categories, Figure 3.1 shows a panel of four charts detailing the cumulative response over 24 weeks to one-standard deviation innovations of: flows to flows (top left), flows to returns (top right), returns to flows (bottom left), and returns to returns (bottom right). The horizontal scale shows time measured in weeks. The vertical scale displays the flows and returns as a percent of the assets in that category at the beginning of the week.

The cumulative response (shown in blue) from the VAR is bracketed in each chart by a two-standard deviation bandwidth (shown in red), where the standard error was estimated from a Monte Carlo simulation of the VAR with 1,000 repetitions. The key evidence for the model feedback loop appears in the top right and bottom left charts of each four-chart panel. For example, consider the panel for emerging market funds showing fund flows (EM_FLOWS) and market returns (EM_MKTCHG). Within 4 weeks, a positive one-standard-deviation innovation in market returns (equaling 0.9 percent) results in a 0.3 percent cumulative increase in emerging market fund inflows as a share of assets (see top right chart in panel). By 24 weeks, the cumulative increase reaches 0.5 percent. The bottom left chart of this panel shows that a positive one-standard-deviation innovation in emerging market fund flows (equaling 1.2 percent of assets) results in an increased return of 0.4 percent that grows over time to 0.6 percent.

---

15. The ordering that puts flows before returns matters only for the HY series; for the other categories reversing the order makes no qualitative difference. We have no *a priori* reason to expect (or *ex-post* explanation for why) the VAR results for the HY category would be more sensitive to this identifying assumption than the others.

	Week 1	Week 2	Week 12	Week 24
UST	-	0.003	0.064	0.065
	-	(0.027)	(0.072)	(0.073)
MBS	-	0.034***	0.332***	0.541***
	-	(0.009)	(0.071)	(0.131)
HY	-	0.131***	0.039	0.011
	-	(0.013)	(0.084)	(0.098)
IG	-	0.037***	0.221***	0.301***
	-	(0.006)	(0.038)	(0.061)
EM	-	0.188***	0.486***	0.511***
	-	(0.026)	(0.139)	(0.157)
EQ	-	0.028***	0.028*	0.028*
	-	(0.006)	(0.014)	(0.015)

Table 3.1. Cumulative Impulse Response of Flows to Returns
(Standard errors in parentheses)

Note: Standard errors are based on a Monte Carlo simulation involving 1,000 repetitions.
*** denotes significance at the 1% confidence threshold, ** denotes significance at the 5% threshold, * denotes
significance at the 10% threshold

A comparable pattern of statistically significant responses – both from flows to returns and returns to flows – is evident in the panels for investment grade funds (IG) and mortgage-backed securities (MBS). For the HY category, the response of returns to flows is significant, but the link between shocks to returns and flows is weak. In each case, the off-diagonal charts (top right and bottom left) show a two-standard-deviation bandwidth.

Tables 3.1 and 3.2 make it easier to see how strong the statistical relationships are. In five of the six categories (excluding Treasuries), the responses of flows to returns are significant at the 1% confidence interval out to two weeks. In four of the six categories (excluding Treasuries and MBS), the responses of returns to flows are significant at the 1% confidence level out to two weeks. In four of the six categories (excluding Treasuries and equities), the response of returns to flows is significant at the 1% or 5% confidence level across most of the 24-week pro-

	Week 1	Week 2	Week 12	Week 24
UST	0.007	0.013	0.014	0.014
	(0.021)	(0.029)	(0.049)	(0.050)
MBS	0.022	0.027	0.083**	0.127**
	(0.013)	(0.017)	(0.036)	(0.061)
HY	0.307***	0.430***	0.514***	0.507***
	(0.020)	(0.035)	(0.112)	(0.123)
IG	0.068***	0.092***	0.183***	0.223***
	(0.016)	(0.022)	(0.057)	(0.085)
EM	0.248***	0.283***	0.555***	0.575***
	(0.039)	(0.058)	(0.184)	(0.211)
EQ	0.601***	0.426***	0.003	0.007
	(0.069)	(0.096)	(0.166)	(0.168)

Table 3.2. Cumulative Impulse Response of Returns to Flows
(Standard errors in parentheses)

Note: Standard errors are based on a Monte Carlo simulation involving 1,000 repetitions.
*** denotes significance at the 1% confidence threshold, ** denotes significance at the 5% confidence threshold,
* denotes significance at the 10% confidence threshold

jection interval. Finally, excluding Treasuries and high yield funds, the response of flows to returns is significant across the 24-week projection interval at the 1% confidence level (or, in the case of equities, at the 10% confidence level). Considering the noisy measurement of the flows and returns, and the volatility evident in the data, the significance of the cumulative equity and high yield responses in Figure 3.1 out to at least four and six weeks, respectively, seems nontrivial. It is consistent with the previous literature on fund behavior showing flows that track performance.

Not surprisingly, the magnitude of these effects is generally largest for the three bond categories that show statistically significant bi-directional influence between flows and returns. While the magnitudes are notable, they also are not so large as to be implausible. Summary statistics for the VARs that generated these impulse response charts and the table are available in the Appendix.

US Treasury Bonds (UST)

Mortgage Backed Securities (MBS)

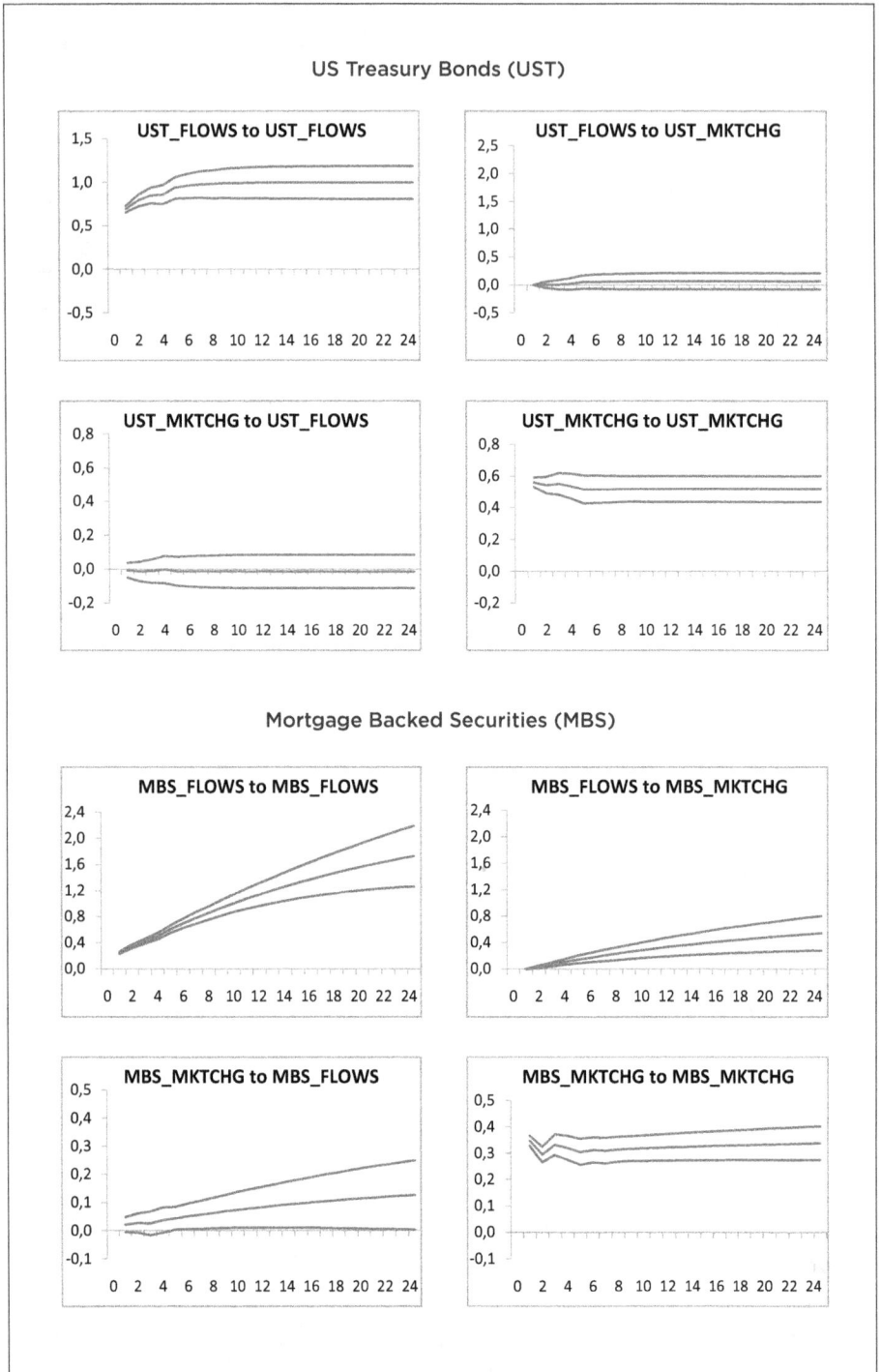

Figure 3.1. Impulse Responses from Estimated Vector Autoregressions
US Treasury Bonds (UST)

High Yield Bonds (HY)

EM_FLOWS to EM_FLOWS

EM_FLOWS to EM_MKTCHG

EM_MKTCHG to EM_FLOWS

EM_MKTCHG to EM_MKTCHG

Investment Grade Bonds (IG)

EQ_FLOWS to EQ_FLOWS

EQ_FLOWS to EQ_MKTCHG

EQ_MKTCHG to EQ_FLOWS

EQ_MKTCHG to EQ_MKTCHG

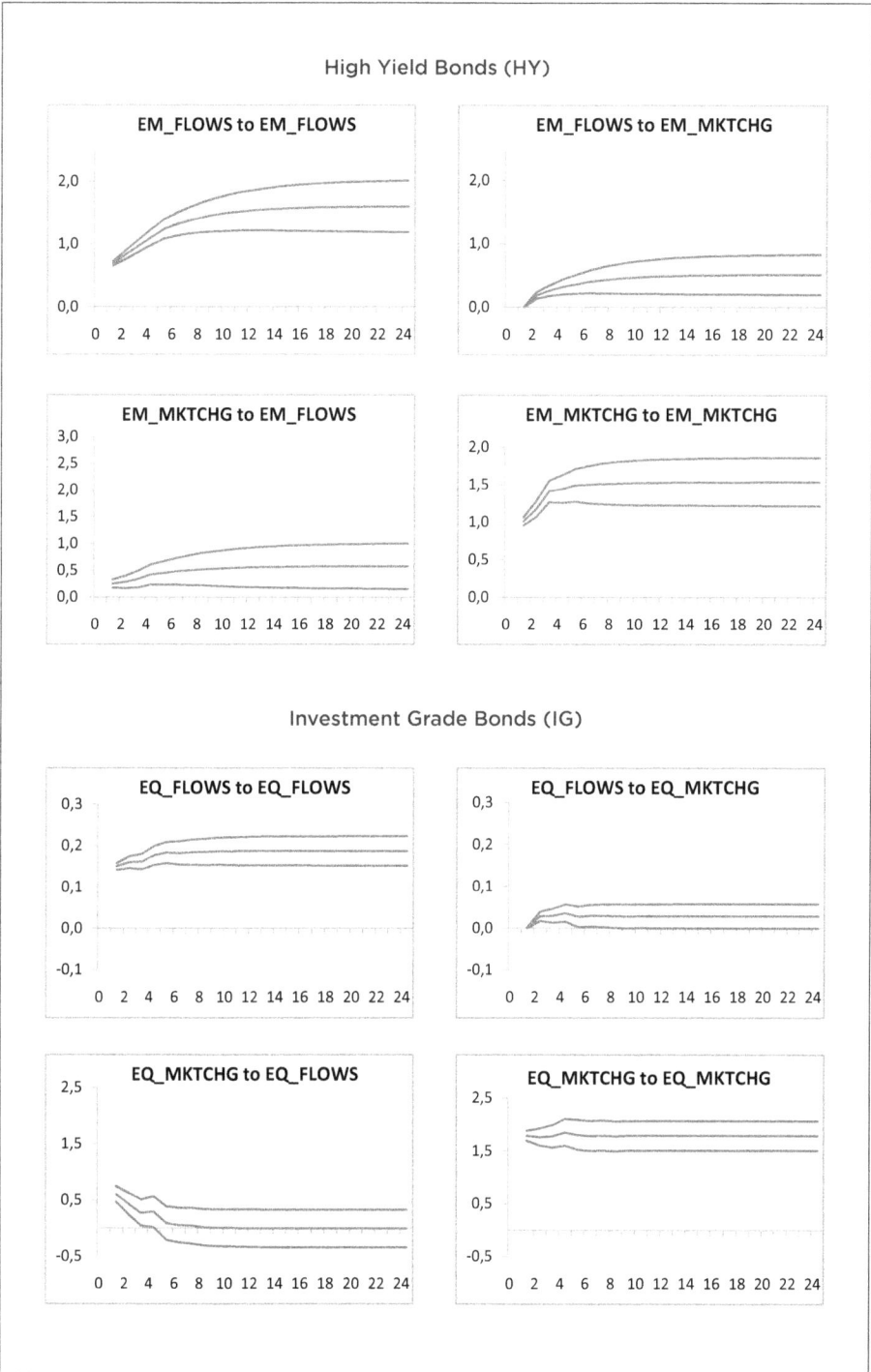

Figure 3.1. (continued)

Emerging Market Bonds (EM)

HY_FLOWS to HY_FLOWS

HY_FLOWS to HY_MKTCHG

HY_MKTCHG to HY_FLOWS

HY_MKTCHG to HY_MKTCHG

Domestic Equities (EQ)

IG_FLOWS to IG_FLOWS

IG_FLOWS to IG_MKTCHG

IG_MKTCHG to IG_FLOWS

IG_MKTCHG to IG_MKTCHG

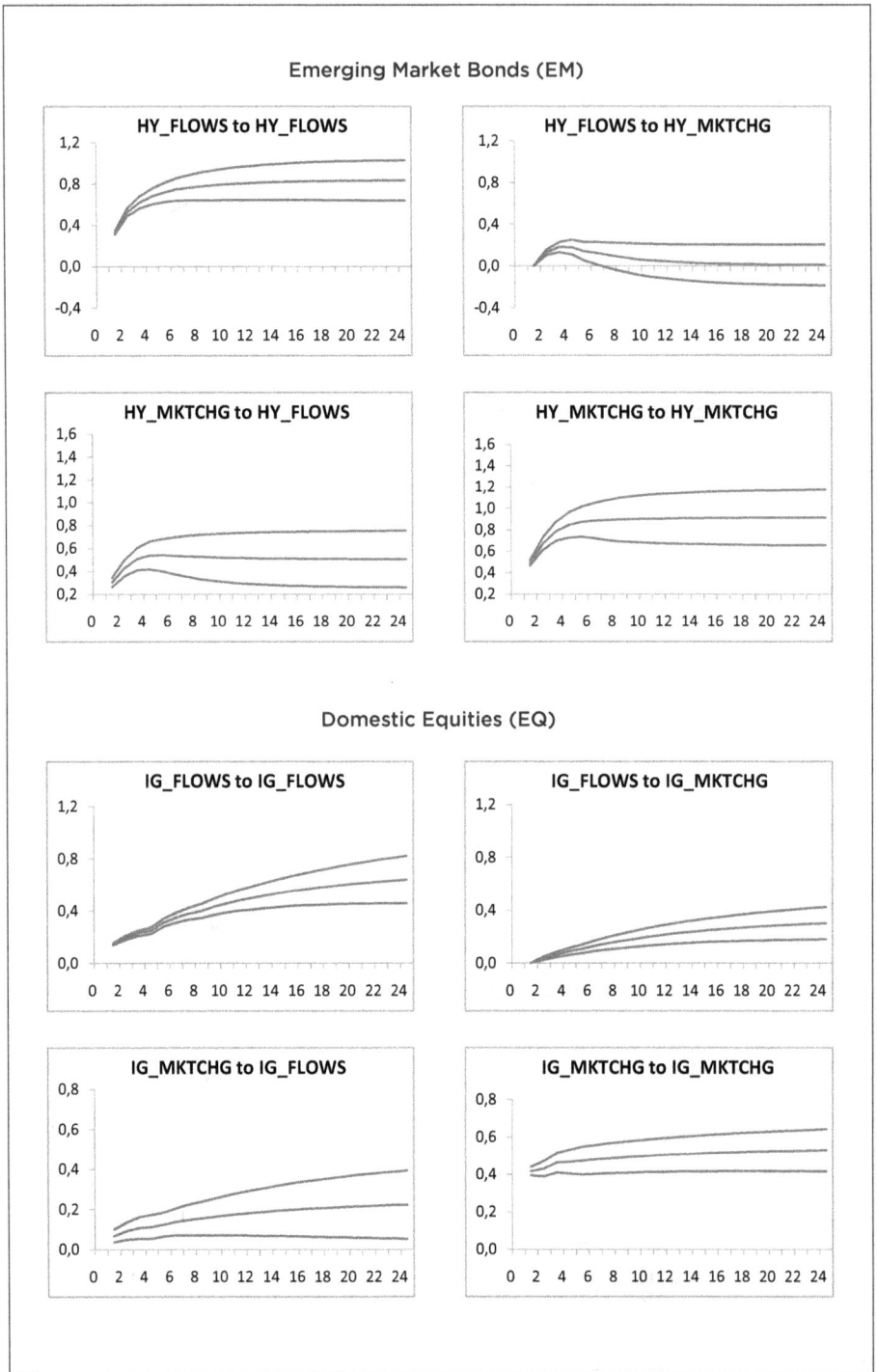

Figure 3.1. (continued)

3.2 Bond Market Sentiment

Having established that the feedback mechanism posited by the model is present, at least for most bond fund categories, we examine the evidence for "risk-on / risk-off" switches in bond market sentiment and turn to the question of how coordinated are the actions of investors. The model suggested one mechanism that creates incentives for investors to chase yields and to prefer to move into a trade sooner rather than later. In this section, we examine more formally the degree to which fund flows are synchronized across asset categories as the model suggests.

Figure 2.4 previously offered informal evidence that common cycles might be present across selected fund types. However, given the disparate characteristics of these assets, one might suspect that flows and returns would not be tightly linked. For instance, hedging motives would be unlikely to explain co-movements between these categories. Figure 3.4 also highlighted that flows do not necessarily coincide in some large macro events such as the Asian crisis in 1997. Consequently, on *a priori* grounds, it is far from obvious that one would expect a high degree of synchronization.

As a first approach, we recorded all the readings where the HY, IG, MBS and EM flows shown in Figure 2.4 (that is, all the bond fund categories excluding Treasuries) were in the upper or lower quarter of the observations. We then overlaid these filtered samples and noted the dates when all of the flows for each category were large and in the same direction (prior to 1995, in light of the measurement concerns with the EM series, we used only the HY, IG and MBS series). We denote these overlap periods as dates of "risk-on" and "risk-off" for the fixed income markets. The dates are shown in Figure 3.2.

We find the picture intriguing. The dates of the synchronized movements match a number of anecdotal accounts of developments in bond markets. In particular, this simple filter picks out several familiar dates when most market commentators would have observed a shift in sentiment. For instance, both the 1994 and 2013 episodes are marked as risk-off periods of heavy fund outflows. The Y2K period is also identified as a risk-off episode. On the other hand, this measure picks out two risk-on episodes. The first, in early 1992, is when the Fed began aggressively cutting interest rates once it determined that the recovery faced serious headwinds. The second occasion was in early 2003, when the Fed had lowered short-term interest rates close to 1 percent. The Fed's first attempt to use forward guidance followed soon after. The other two risk-off periods are in mid-2004, when the Fed began raising interest rates for the first time in five years, and mid-2006, around the last time that the Fed raised interest rates.

While this indicator is interesting, it is ad hoc and suffers from several obvious drawbacks, such as equally weighting the four underlying time series and ignoring magnitudes. Consequently, in the remainder of our analysis, we utilize a more conventional statistical proxy for the co-movement of bond fund flows; namely, we extract the first principal component of normalized flows in Figure 2.3 for the four bond fund classes excluding Treasuries: namely, HY, IG, MBS, and EM.

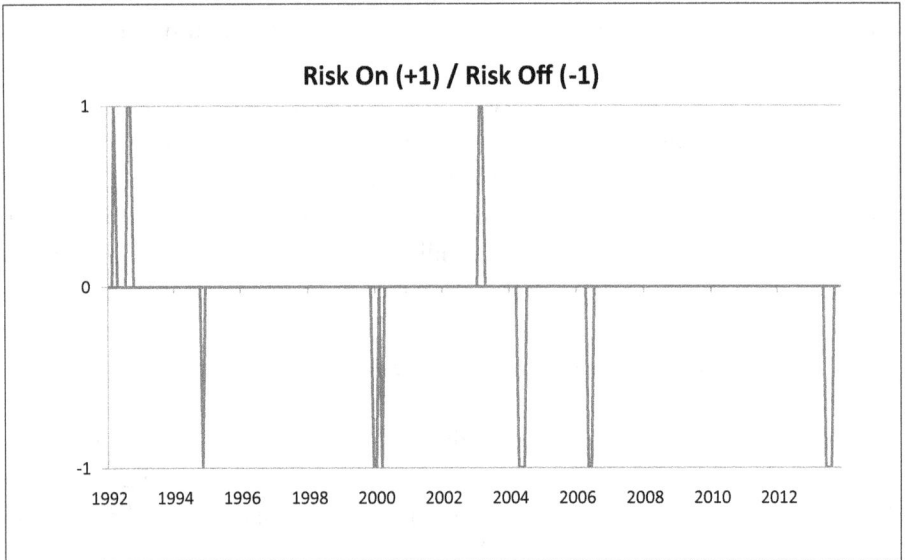

Figure 3.2. Risk On / Risk Off Dates in Fixed Income Markets

Principal component analysis transforms the original collection of random variables into a set of orthogonal series. The first principal component is selected to explain the maximum amount of the variance of the original data series. Loosely speaking, it can be thought of as the dominant common factor that is present in the data set. We refer to this first component as our bond market sentiment indicator. In this application, the sentiment indicator explains just under half the overall variance of the normalized flows and it is graphed in Figure 3.3. For comparison, in the top panel of Figure 3.3, we also show the risk-on/risk off indicator from Figure 3.2.

Because the first principal component seeks to account for as much variance as possible, this sentiment index should pick up large common movements across the fund categories. This component puts relatively similar weights on each of the four input series. Hence, it could be sensitive to large idiosyncratic swings in one or two series. Likewise, there is no mechanical reason why the first principal component should be nearly as binary as the risk-on/risk off proxy. In short, this statistical procedure does not ensure that the first principal component will serve as a plausible sentiment proxy.

First Principal Component - Fixed Income Flows

First Principal Component - Fixed Income Flows

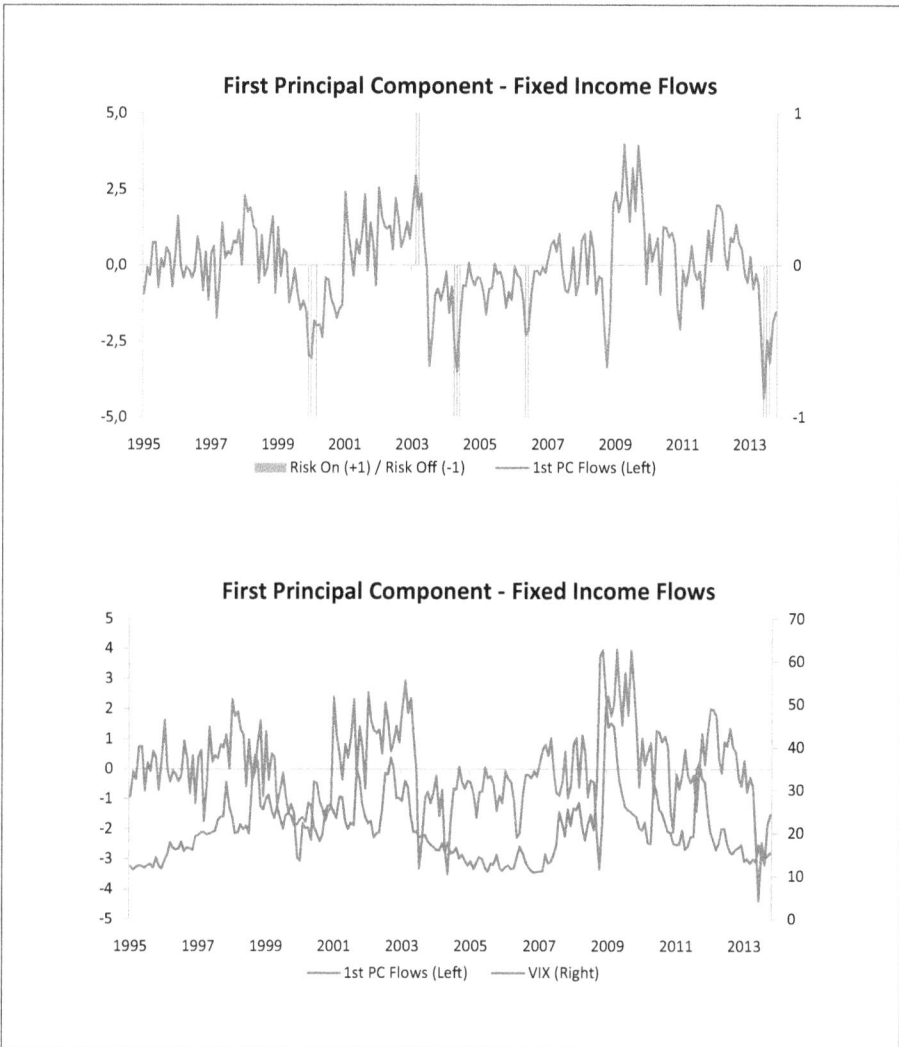

Figure 3.3. Bond Market Sentiment Indicator, Risk On/Risk Off Proxy and the VIX

Despite these potential caveats, the first principal component looks like a useful sentiment indicator. Two characteristics of the indicator are noteworthy. First, it exhibits some very abrupt swings. The top panel shows that many of these shifts occur around the time intervals that were picked out by our informal indicators and that we already tied to anecdotal information. However, this more formal measure also highlights several other occasions involving big improvements or declines in sentiment. These include the sentiment collapse following the Lehman Brothers bankruptcy and the recovery that followed in the spring of 2009 when the U.S. Supervisory Capital Assessment Program results were announced and the economy started to emerge from the recession. Of course, there also are other movements that are less easy to tie to specific events.

Second, the lower panel of Figure 3.3 shows that our sentiment indicator is not merely a relabeling of the VIX. As Rey (2013) and others have noted, the VIX has remarkable predictive power for many other financial and nonfinancial macroeconomic variables. However, the theory underlying the model in this paper suggests that we are trying to capture something more than just the volatility of equity markets. Consequently, it is reassuring that our measure seems to have done that. Moreover, these differences with the VIX imply that the role of the sentiment indicator that we explore in the next section cannot be viewed merely as the impact of a VIX proxy. Put differently, the results do not represent a mere repackaging of information that is known from previous studies of the VIX.

As a companion to the sentiment indicator, we also extract the first principal component of the returns that were shown in Figure 2.5. For comparison, the top panel of Figure 3.4 shows it along with the risk on/risk off indicator, while the bottom panel shows the principal component along with the VIX.

We draw two main conclusions from Figure 3.4. First, the common movements in prices are much less volatile than the movements of the individual components: note how much less choppy this figure is than the components in Figure 2.5. Nevertheless, the percentage of the total variance explained by the first principal component is above 60 percent. Second, the price movements do not closely track either the VIX or the risk-on/risk off proxy. In particular, although the Lehman period dominates the movements in both the VIX and the return series, the overall correlation between the VIX and the first principal component of returns is only -0.08. Once again, the price movements are not very predictable using the VIX.

3.3 Monetary Policy and Bond Market Sentiment

Finally, we turn to the central hypothesis of interest. The model in section 1 predicts that monetary policy shocks can prompt large shifts in bond market sentiment that move both flows and returns. The model also suggests that the larger and more persistent the fund inflows, the larger the reversal (in flows and returns) in the face of a big monetary policy shock. Put differently, a large cumulation of return-driving fund inflows – partly in response to monetary accommodation – sets the stage for a sharp outflow when policy shifts direction.[16]

---

16.   Once again, other models – such as one driven by redemptions – could imply a responsiveness to monetary policy shocks. Our empirical work in this paper does not distinguish between alternative yield-chasing models.

To assess these hypotheses, we estimate a three-variable VAR that includes flows, returns and monetary policy surprises. The results of the experiment are consistent with two key implications of the model: namely, policy can drive flows, and flows can drive prices.

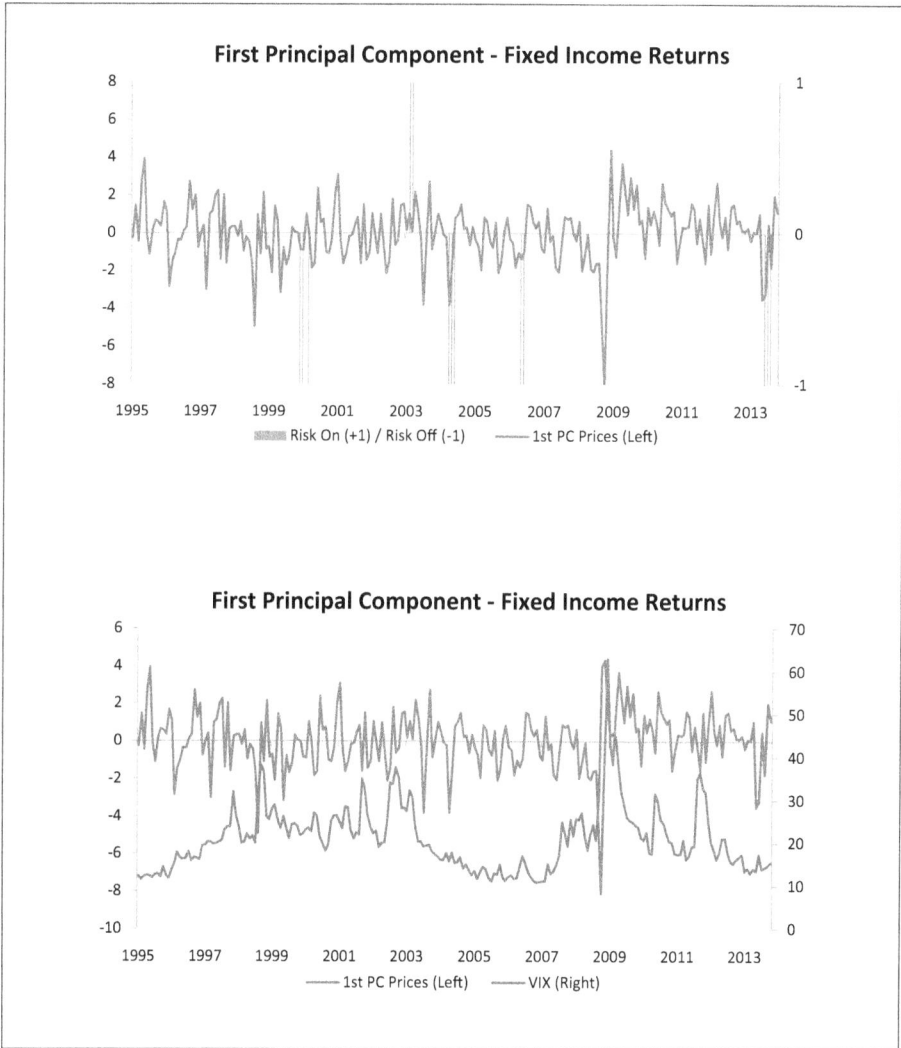

Figure 3.4. First Principal Component of Fixed Income Securities Returns

In a period of zero policy interest rates, forward guidance and large changes of the central bank's balance sheet, there is no single optimal indicator of monetary policy surprises. In this section, we use a measure from Stehn and Hatzius (2012)

that was constructed in the spirit of Wright (2012), who exploits the heteroske-dasticity in daily-frequency data (along with the known dates of policy announcements) to identify monetary policy shocks at the zero bound in a structural VAR. The Stehn-Hatzius version extends the Wright shock series, which begins in 2008, back to 2001. We then compare this variable to the principal components for returns and flows that were displayed in Figures 3.3 and 3.4.

The VAR is estimated on a monthly basis from July 2001 through October 2013. It includes three lags each of the monetary policy shock, the first principal component of the four flows and the first principal component of the four returns. The Cholesky ordering places the policy shock first, consistent with its postulated exogeneity. As in Section 3.1, the ordering also puts flows before returns, consistent with the model's emphasis on flows as drivers. Summary statistics of the VAR are provided in the Appendix.

Figures 3.5 and 3.6 each show panels of nine figures that characterize the impulse responses from the VAR. Figure 3.5 exhibits the instantaneous response of each VAR component to a one-standard-deviation shock in the monetary policy shock (labeled WRIGHT, column 1), in the first principal component of flows (labeled FLOWFOUR1, column 2), and in the first principal component of returns (labeled PRICEFOUR1, column 3). Figure 3.6 shows the accumulated responses over time. In each chart, time is measured in months along the horizontal axis, while the units on the vertical axis are in percentage points for the WRIGHT shock and percent of assets for the others. The blue line denotes the projected response, while the red lines enclose a two-standard deviation bandwidth around that projection. As before, the standard errors are based on a 1000-repetition Monte Carlo estimate. Statistical significance (at the 5% confidence interval) is evident when the red bands enclosing the projection are both on one side of the zero mark.

Figure 3.5 highlights four conclusions from this experiment:

- A surprise tightening of monetary policy prompts early, and statistically significant, negative responses in the first principal components of both flows and returns (column 1, rows 2 and 3). The restrictive effect remains statistically significant for up to three months.
- The first principal component of flows does not respond in a statistically significant way to an innovation in the first principal component of returns (column 3, row 2). This absence may reflect other shocks within the month that mask the patterns we saw in the weekly data. Another possibility is that some portion of the common movement in the four bond funds has been picked up in higher-order principal components.
- Returns show a positive and statistically significant response for two months in response to an innovation in the first principal component of flows (column 2, row 3).

- The impulse responses of the monetary policy shocks to all of the innovations are transient, as one would expect in light of the way that these shocks were identified.

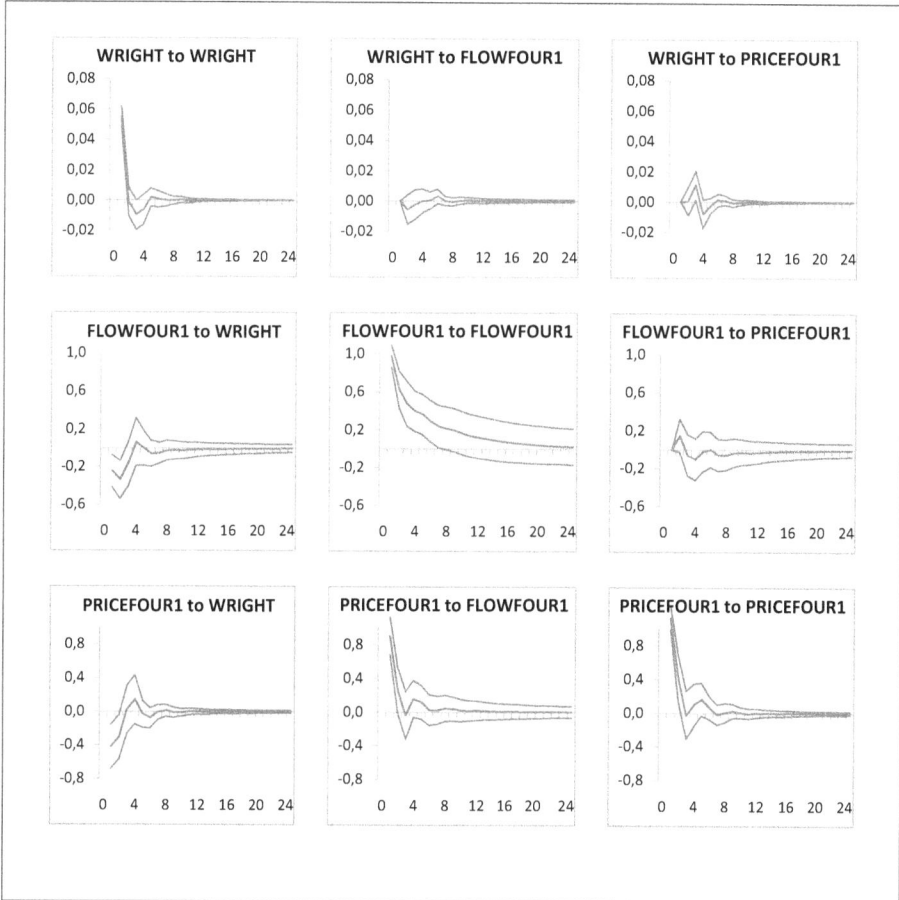

Figure 3.5. Monthly VAR Impulse Responses

Figure 3.6 confirms that these responses for returns and flows do not reverse (although statistical significance weakens after a few months).

Cohen and Shin (2002) employed a similar VAR approach to study how price changes are related to net sales by market participants. Using high-frequency data for the trading of U.S. Treasury securities, they found that net sales are stabilizing during normal times, but that during more turbulent trading episodes, net sales and price changes tend to amplify each other. In other words, during normal times, when prices fall, net purchases by investors cushion the price fall.

However, during turbulent trading episodes, price declines lead to increased net sales, leading to further declines. In this way, price dynamics and trading tend to amplify shocks during turbulent episodes.

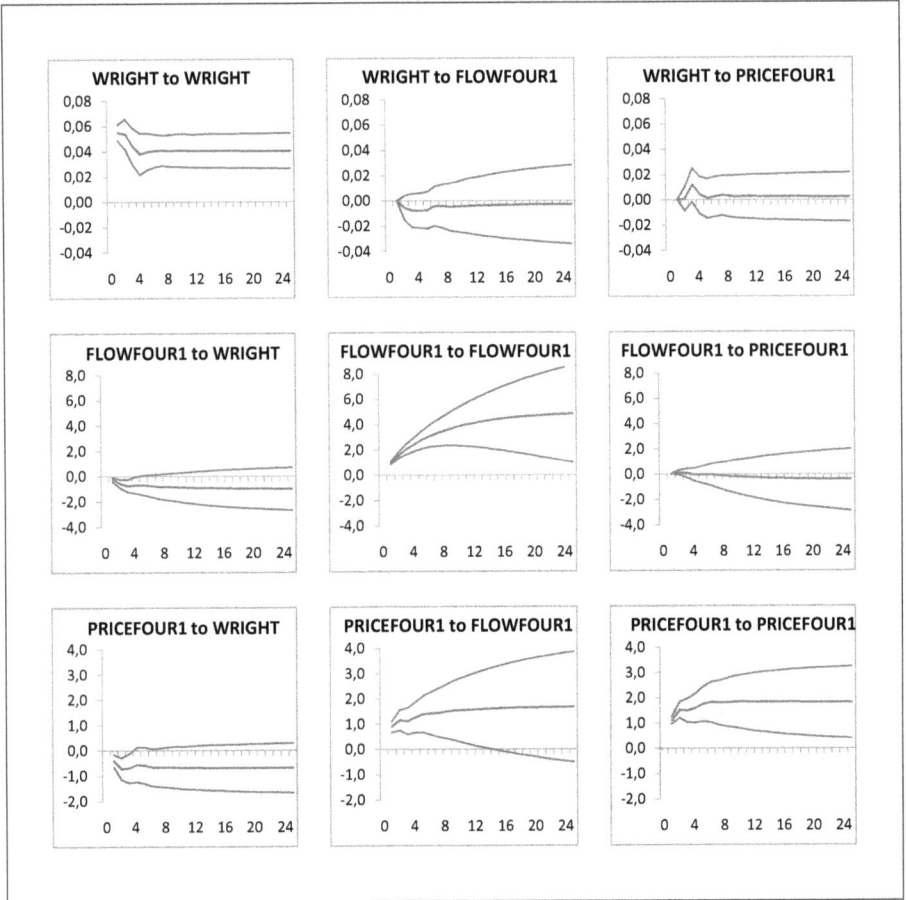

Figure 3.6. Accumulated Monthly Impulse Responses

For the funds examined in our paper, the results line up more closely with the amplifying episodes examined in Cohen and Shin (2002). We therefore view the results of the experiment as being consistent with the key implications of our model: namely, monetary shocks can drive flows, and flows can drive prices.

Overall, our empirical results support the theoretical mechanism outlined in our simple model. In contrast to textbook long-term investors who step into a falling market to cushion price falls, the evidence from bond fund flows shows the potential for amplifying interactions of price and quantity changes.

As we described in earlier sections, our results also are consistent with the potential magnifying effects of redemption pressures arising from fund investors facing run-like incentives. The evidence on fund flows cannot discriminate between these alternative theoretical mechanisms. In any case, the existence of run-like incentives generated by redemption pressures would reinforce the transmission channels put forward in our paper.

4. Conclusions

Rather than rehashing the main findings, we conclude by putting the results in a broader context and addressing several questions that the analysis opens up.

Perhaps most important is the question of whether the 2013 episode was a one-time anomaly or a realization of an important risk associated with the unconventional policies that were implemented following the crisis. To be sure, in the wake of the summer 2013 taper tantrum, the U.S. economy registered the strongest half-year GDP growth since 2005. Nevertheless, our view is that there is sufficient justification for policymakers to factor in the risks to the real economy associated with a market tantrum when setting monetary policy.

For example, Figure 4.1 shows the Adjusted National Financial Conditions Index (ANFCI) produced each week by the Federal Reserve Bank of Chicago from 1985 to the present. This index is the first principal component from 105 financial market indicators. The index is normalized so that its average value is zero and its standard deviation of 1. The adjusted index controls for inflation and the state of the business cycle (see Brave and Kelley (2017)) to try to isolate the purely financial information from the series. Despite the jump in Treasury bond yields in the mid-2013 market tantrum, the ANFCI chart shows that overall financial conditions remained quite loose—with financial stress much lower than normal—helping to explain the resilience of the economy.

Perhaps more remarkable, overall financial conditions remained loose well after the Federal Reserve began raising its policy rate (in December 2015) and began shrinking its balance sheet (in October 2017). As of spring 2018, financial stress is still below the long-run norm. This almost surely reflects an intentional policy choice by the Federal Reserve that probably has helped avoid a replay of the 2013 tantrum. In our view, this is no small achievement. However, until policy reaches a neutral or restrictive stance, it would be premature to conclude that another tantrum has been definitely avoided.

Another issue raised by our analysis is how to model the impact of bond market tantrums on the economy. Our very simple model boils this down to three parameters. The first is the size of the selling that happens when investors exit a trade.

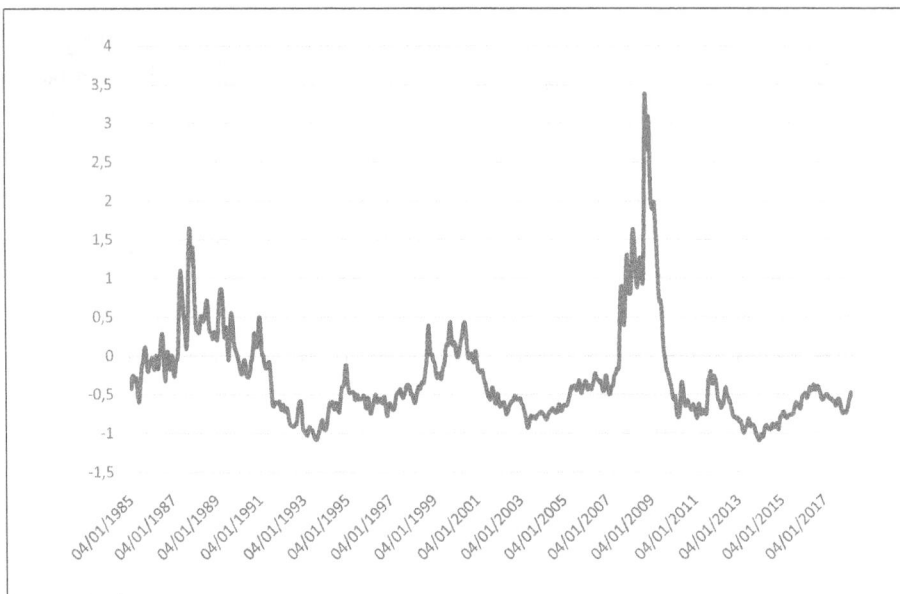

Figure 4.1. Federal Reserve Bank of Chicago's Adjusted National
Financial Conditions Index

The prospective scale of selling could perhaps be calibrated by using the buildup in positions over time, but this stockpiling is not the kind of indicator that is normally tracked by policy makers or market analysts.

The second input in the calculation would be the pass through from selling to other market interest rates. This elasticity is a particularly difficult one to deduce. Markets are continuously evolving, and so is the risk-bearing capacity of the residual buyers of securities who would have to step in during a large selloff by delegated managers. Conceptually, however, we would like to know what happens to interest rates if X billion dollars of assets were dumped in a short time interval by investors? There is not much evidence to address this important question.

The third and final component of the calculation is the interest sensitivity of investment and consumption. These parameters are also difficult to estimate, but are the subject of many empirical investigations.[17] Moreover, estimates of these effects are present in most macroeconomic models so that this piece of the calculation likely would be the least controversial of the three.

Finally, there are many ways in which the sentiment index could be extended and improved. It would be natural to incorporate other risk classes to expand the

---

17. For example, see Zwick and Mahon (2014) Appendix 2 for a survey of the investment elasticity with respect to interest rates.

investigation. For instance, adding carry trades that involve government bonds in different markets would be a natural addition to the index. It might also make sense to look at commodity markets. Besides the inclusion of other asset classes, it might also be fruitful to include the behavior of funds and asset managers outside the United States. The investigation in this report is only a first step in looking at these risks.

One main takeaway that we hope to convey is that simply looking at price indicators is insufficient for assessing financial stability. In that sense, we think the biggest lesson from the last crisis is that investors and policymakers should track quantity positions for their own sake. To learn about these risks depends partly on understanding who owns which assets and how those positions may have been hedged with other instruments. Unfortunately, we do not have very good information on the concentration of ownership (across borders or for different types of assets). More basic measurement on this front would be very welcome.

REFERENCES

Becker, Bo and Victoria Ivashina, 2013, "Reaching for Yield in the Bond Market" National Bureau of Economic Research Working Paper No. 18909.

Borio, Claudio and Haibin Zhu, 2012, "Capital regulation, risk-taking and monetary policy: a missing link in the transmission mechanism?" BIS working paper 268 and *Journal of Financial Stability*, 8(4), 236-251.

Brave, Scott A. and David Kelly, 2017, "Introducing the Chicago Fed's New Adjusted National Financial Conditions Index", *Chicago Fed Letter*, No. 386, 2017.

Chen, Qi, Itay Goldstein and Wei Jiang, 2010, "Payoff complementarities and financial fragility: Evidence from mutual fund outflows", *Journal of Financial Economics* 97 (2), 239-262

Chevalier, Judith A. and Glenn Ellison, 1997, "Risk Taking by Mutual Funds as a Response to Incentives," *Journal of Political Economy*, vol. 105(6), pp. 1176-1200.

Cohen, Benjamin H. and Hyun Song Shin, 2002, "Positive feedback trading in the US treasury market" BIS Quarterly Review 7 (2), 59-67.

Diamond Douglas and Philip Dybvig, 1983, "Bank Runs, Deposit Insurance, and Liquidity" *Journal of Political Economy*, 91, 401-19.

Gertler, Mark, and Peter Karadi. 2015. "Monetary Policy Surprises, Credit Costs, and Economic Activity." *American Economic Journal: Macroeconomics*, 7 (1): 44-76.

Greenlaw, David, Hatzius, Jan, Kashyap Anil K and Hyun Song Shin, 2008, "Leveraged Losses: Lessons from the Mortgage Market Meltdown", U.S. Monetary Policy Forum Report No. 2, Rosenberg Institute, Brandeis International Business School and Initiative on Global Markets, University of Chicago Graduate School of Business.

Hanson, Samuel and Jeremy C. Stein, 2012, "Monetary Policy and Long-Term Real Rates." Harvard Business School Working Paper, No. 13-008

Kocherlakota, Narayana, 2013, "Low Real Interest Rates", Remarks at the 22nd Annual Hyman P. Minsky Conference, Levy Economics Institute of Bard College, New York, New York April 18, 2013

Morris, Stephen and Hyun Song Shin, 2014, "The Risk-Taking Channel of Monetary Policy: A Global Game Approach" working paper

Office of Financial Research, 2013, *Annual Report to Congress*, Washington, DC. http://www.treasury.gov/initiatives/ofr/about/Documents/OFR_AnnualReport2013_FINAL_12-17-2013_Accessible.pdf

Rajan, Raghuram, 2005, "Has financial development made the world riskier?", paper presented at Federal Reserve Bank of Kansas City Symposium at Jackson Hole, Wyoming, August 25-27.

Rey, Helene, 2013, "Dilemma not Trilemma: The Global Financial Cycle and Monetary Policy Independence", Federal Reserve Bank of Kansas City Jackson Hole Economic Policy Symposium, *Global Dimensions of Unconventional Monetary Policy*, pp. 285-333.

Shiller, Robert J., John Y. Campbell, and Kermit L. Schoenholtz, 1983, "Forward Rates and Future Policy: Interpreting the Term Structure of Interest Rates," *Brookings Papers on Economic Activity*, Vol. 1983, No. 1, 173-223.

Shin, Hyun Song, 2013, "Second Phase of Global Liquidity and Its Impact on Emerging Economies", keynote address as the Federal Reserve Bank of San Francisco's Asia Economic Policy Conference, http://www.princeton.edu/~hsshin/www/FRBSF_2013.pdf

Sven Jari Stehn and Jan Hatzius, "Monetary Policy and the GSFCI," *US Economics Analyst*, Goldman Sachs, June 29, 2012.

Jeremy C. Stein, 2014, "Incorporating Financial Stability Considerations into a Monetary Policy Framework" speech at the International Research Forum on Monetary Policy, Washington, D.C. https://www.federalreserve.gov/newsevents/speech/stein20140321a.htm

Tucker, Paul, 2014, "Regulatory Reform, Stability, and Central Banking", report of the Hutchins Center on Fiscal and Monetary Policy, Brookings Institution.

Turner, Philip, 2014, "The global long-term interest rate, financial risks and policy choices in EMEs" BIS working paper 441, https://www.bis.org/publ/work441.htm

Vayanos, Dimitri and Paul Woolley, 2013, "An Institutional Theory of Momentum and Reversal", *Review of Financial Studies*, 2013, 26, 1087-1145.

Wright, Jonathan, 2012, "What does Monetary Policy do to Long-term Interest Rates at the Zero Lower Bound?", *Economic Journal* , vol. 122 (2012), pp.F447-F466.

Zwick, Eric and James Mahon, 2014, "Do Financial Frictions Amplify Fiscal Policy? Evidence from Business Investment Stimulus", working paper.

APPENDIX

Supporting Information for Section 3.1 Bivariate VARs

Sample (adjusted): 2/11/1998 to 12/11/2013
Included observations: 706 after adjustments
Standard errors in parentheses

US Treasuries (UST)

	UST_FLOWS	UST_MKTCHG
UST_FLOWS(-1)	0.140381***	-0.008954
	(0.03600)	(0.02910)
UST_FLOWS(-2)	0.05922*	0.004442
	(0.03454)	(0.02792)
UST_FLOWS(-3)	-0.002856	0.011593
	(0.03372)	(0.02726)
UST_FLOWS(-4)	0.107641***	-0.015227
	(0.03228)	(0.02609)
UST_MKTCHG(-1)	0.006192	-0.034343
	(0.04680)	(0.03783)
UST_MKTCHG(-2)	-0.000627	0.012659
	(0.04706)	(0.03804)
UST_MKTCHG(-3)	0.025065	-0.024055
	(0.04706)	(0.03804)
UST_MKTCHG(-4)	0.056924	-0.038345
	(0.04780)	(0.03863)
@MSUM(UST_LIPPER_FLOWS_CL(-1),104)/ UST_LIPPER	0.357217***	0.094203
_ASSETS_CL(-105)	(0.11929)	(0.09642)
C	0.047646	0.034839
	(0.03707)	(0.02997)
R-squared	0.083099	0.005227
Adj. R-squared	0.071243	-0.007636

(*, **, and *** indicates significance at 10%, 5%, and 1% confidence threshold)

Mortgage-backed Securities (MBS)

	MBS_FLOWS	MBS_MKTCHG
MBS_FLOWS(-1)	0.392393***	0.035665
	(0.03708)	(0.05236)
MBS_FLOWS(-2)	0.163053***	-0.024241
	(0.03962)	(0.05594)
MBS_FLOWS(-3)	0.100894**	0.0439
	(0.03939)	(0.05562)
MBS_FLOWS(-4)	0.225983***	0.020013
	(0.03708)	(0.05236)
MBS_MKTCHG(-1)	0.098655***	-0.149353***
	(0.02663)	(0.03760)
MBS_MKTCHG(-2)	0.077325***	0.081548**
	(0.02722)	(0.03843)
MBS_MKTCHG(-3)	0.06177**	-0.008744
	(0.02788)	(0.03936)
MBS_MKTCHG(-4)	0.032166	-0.064834
	(0.02869)	(0.04051)
@MSUM(UST_LIPPER_FLOWS_CL(-1),104)/ UST_LIPPER	-0.023524	-0.007841
_ASSETS_CL(-105)	(0.04014)	(0.05668)
C	-0.006582	0.054805***
	(0.00986)	(0.01392)
R-squared	0.669936	0.041276
Adj. R-squared	0.665668	0.028879

(*, **, and *** indicates significance at 10%, 5%, and 1% confidence threshold)

High-yield Securities (HY)

	HY_FLOWS	HY_MKTCHG
HY_FLOWS(-1)	0.359612***	0.035928
	(0.04398)	(0.07767)
HY_FLOWS(-2)	0.056948	-0.00476
	(0.04661)	(0.08232)
HY_FLOWS(-3)	0.083234*	-0.040065
	(0.04574)	(0.08078)
HY_FLOWS(-4)	0.10482***	-0.032639
	(0.03906)	(0.06899)
HY_MKTCHG(-1)	0.265452***	0.364442***
	(0.02535)	(0.04477)
HY_MKTCHG(-2)	-0.092499***	0.087045*
	(0.02751)	(0.04858)
HY_MKTCHG(-3)	-0.080168***	0.005161
	(0.02752)	(0.04860)
HY_MKTCHG(-4)	-0.088926***	0.005967
	(0.02746)	(0.04850)
@MSUM(UST_LIPPER_FLOWS_CL(-1),104)/ UST_LIPPER	0.105411	0.187695
_ASSETS_CL(-105)	(0.07691)	(0.13583)
C	0.024337	-0.01681
	(0.01645)	(0.02905)
R-squared	0.425944	0.174802
Adj. R-squared	0.418521	0.164131

(*, **, and *** indicates significance at 10%, 5%, and 1% confidence threshold)

Investment-grade Securities (IG)

	IG_FLOWS	IG_MKTCHG
IG_FLOWS(-1)	0.285232***	0.149444
	(0.03476)	(0.10009)
IG_FLOWS(-2)	0.106948***	0.024017
	(0.03575)	(0.10295)
IG_FLOWS(-3)	0.004518	-0.018686
	(0.03513)	(0.10117)
IG_FLOWS(-4)	0.337044***	0.061614
	(0.03279)	(0.09441)
IG_MKTCHG(-1)	0.088725***	0.032049
	(0.01337)	(0.03850)
IG_MKTCHG(-2)	0.034316**	0.061418
	(0.01371)	(0.03949)
IG_MKTCHG(-3)	0.023167*	-0.003313
	(0.01393)	(0.04010)
IG_MKTCHG(-4)	0.020482	0.000884
	(0.01406)	(0.04048)
@MSUM(UST_LIPPER_FLOWS_CL(-1),104)/ UST_LIPPER	-0.029051	-0.075797
_ASSETS_CL(-105)	(0.04993)	(0.14379)
C	0.044652***	0.01352
	(0.01279)	(0.03684)
R-squared	0.494082	0.017354
Adj. R-squared	0.48754	0.004648

(*, **, and *** indicates significance at 10%, 5%, and 1% confidence threshold)

Emerging Market Bonds (EMBONDS)

	EMBOND_FLOWS	EMBOND_MKTCHG
EMBOND_FLOWS(-1)	0.146454***	-0.009897
	(0.03818)	(0.05765)
EMBOND_FLOWS(-2)	0.156365***	-0.00346
	(0.03903)	(0.05893)
EMBOND_FLOWS(-3)	0.128797***	0.117157**
	(0.03944)	(0.05955)
EMBOND_FLOWS(-4)	0.080193**	-0.011805
	(0.03702)	(0.05590)
EMBOND_MKTCHG(-1)	0.18575***	0.165813***
	(0.02565)	(0.03873)
EMBOND_MKTCHG(-2)	0.012968	0.207833***
	(0.02654)	(0.04007)
EMBOND_MKTCHG(-3)	-0.026806	-0.043968
	(0.02670)	(0.04032)
EMBOND_MKTCHG(-4)	-0.009587	-0.016207
	(0.02675)	(0.04038)
@MSUM(UST_LIPPER_FLOWS_CL(-1),104)/ UST_LIPPER	0.135329**	-0.114599
_ASSETS_CL(-105)	(0.06356)	(0.09596)
C	0.048597	0.07724
	(0.03441)	(0.05195)
R-squared	0.260851	0.086393
Adj. R-squared	0.251293	0.074579

(*, **, and *** indicates significance at 10%, 5%, and 1% confidence threshold)

Domestic Equities (DOMEQ)

	DOMEQ_FLOWS	DOMEQ_MKTCHG
DOMEQ_FLOWS(-1)	0.004174	-1.109053**
	(0.03971)	(0.49946)
DOMEQ_FLOWS(-2)	0.023442	-1.044495**
	(0.03959)	(0.49790)
DOMEQ_FLOWS(-3)	0.102953***	-0.035661
	(0.03931)	(0.49432)
DOMEQ_FLOWS(-4)	0.069362*	-1.057671**
	(0.03826)	(0.48119)
DOMEQ_MKTCHG(-1)	0.01542***	-0.013796
	(0.00311)	(0.03914)
DOMEQ_MKTCHG(-2)	0.001031	0.024946
	(0.00319)	(0.04011)
DOMEQ_MKTCHG(-3)	0.003265	0.059821
	(0.00315)	(0.03956)
DOMEQ_MKTCHG(-4)	-0.007196**	-0.019258
	(0.00310)	(0.03898)
@MSUM(UST_LIPPER_FLOWS_CL(-1),104)/ UST_LIPPER	0.290002***	0.030753
_ASSETS_CL(-105)	(0.10018)	(1.25990)
C	0.015182**	0.195448**
	(0.00755)	(0.09498)
R-squared	0.075942	0.032344
Adj. R-squared	0.063993	0.019831

(*, **, and *** indicates significance at 10%, 5%, and 1% confidence threshold)

Supporting Material for Section 3.3 Three-variable VAR

Sample (adjusted): 2001M7 to 2013M10

Included observations: 148 after adjustments

Standard errors in parentheses

	WRIGHT	FLOWFOUR1	PRICEFOUR1
WRIGHT(-1)	-0.044869	-2.809183*	-3.145427
	(0.0862)	(1.57866)	(2.34933)
WRIGHT(-2)	-0.16922*	0.616288	1.012599
	(0.08782)	(1.60837)	(2.39355)
WRIGHT(-3)	-0.147693*	2.986124*	2.604782
	(0.08733)	(1.59937)	(2.38014)
FLOWFOUR1(-1)	-0.00616	0.518742***	-0.075595
	(0.00605)	(0.11084)	(0.16495)
FLOWFOUR1(-2)	-0.008478	0.256607**	0.028417
	(0.0068)	(0.12454)	(0.18534)
FLOWFOUR1(-3)	0.013395**	0.044847	0.072538
	(0.00566)	(0.10373)	(0.15437)
PRICEFOUR1(-1)	0.00054	0.130047*	0.36788***
	(0.00408)	(0.07468)	(0.11114)
PRICEFOUR1(-2)	0.0105**	-0.166756**	-0.144729
	(0.00426)	(0.07804)	(0.11613)
PRICEFOUR1(-3)	-0.00953**	-0.007355	0.170071
	(0.0039)	(0.0715)	(0.1064)
C	-0.002932	-0.010279	0.000358
	(0.00455)	(0.08325)	(0.12389)
R-squared	0.106558	0.564725	0.165171
Adj. R-squared	0.04829	0.536337	0.110726

(*, **, and *** indicates significance at 10%, 5%, and 1% confidence threshold)

Note: WRIGHT is the Wright monetary policy shock. FLOWFOUR1 and PRICEFOUR1 are the first principal components of flows and returns, respectively.

COMMENTS

By Narayana Kocherlakota

Thank, Rick, and thanks to the organizers for inviting me to discuss this very stimulating paper. So I will start with a standard disclaimer. The views I'm going to be expressing in this discussion are my own and they are not necessarily shared by anyone else in the Federal Reserve System and especially my colleagues on the Federal Open Market Committee, and I notice there's several of them here today to confirm that. I want to also thank Ron Feldman, Terry Fitzgerald, Sam Schul-hofer-Wohl, Kei-Mu Yi for very useful comments.

I take the motivation for the Monetary Policy Report to be something that is talked about a lot, that accommodative monetary policy can create the risk of financial instability. Kim's last slide he made reference to the separation principle, and I am certainly a subscriber to the separation principle that it is preferable to mitigate such risks using supervisory tools. But I have to admit that in reality either because of imperfections in those tools or imperfections of the use of those tools, supervision may leave behind residual systemic risk. And this is especially true, I think, given the kinds of risks described in this year's Monetary Policy Report. I think the authors make a compelling case along those lines. The question becomes how should this residual risk, after the application of appropriate supervisory tools, affect monetary policy?

I found I could not talk about this topic of connecting monetary policy with financial stability without some kind of framework. I wasn't able to rely on a purely instinctual approach to drawing those two elements together. So I'm going to present a framework that incorporates systemic risk mitigation into monetary policy making. The main theme here is going to be that systemic risk is going to create a mean variance trade-off for policy. Put differently, it creates a trade-off of risk versus return in some sense. And then I'm going to talk about the lessons from this Monetary Policy Report in light of this framework. I will close with some conclusions.

The framework I'm going to formulate supposes that the monetary policymakers' goals is to set some kind of gap (that I will call X) equal to 0. The interpretation of X will differ depending on the circumstances. For instance, X could equal inflation minus the target, it could equal output minus a sufficient level, employment minus some kind of appropriate level or some combination of the above. The main thing you want to be keeping in mind is that the monetary policymaker wants to set that gap equal to 0 and by increasing some level of accommodation A, the monetary policymaker is going to increase X. So if you think about inflation minus target as the goal, then making monetary policy more accommodative will move inflation higher. Now the problem, of course, is that the policy affects the system with a lag. So after the monetary policymaker acts, the gap is going to be affected by a large number of shocks including potential shocks to the financial system. The central banker's problem is that deviations of the gap from 0 on either side are undesirable. One way to summarize this very simply is that the monetary policymaker suffers a loss such as given by the square of the gap.

Remember the square function. As you move away from 0, the loss gets bigger and bigger and bigger and that's bad. The losses are also symmetric, positive gaps are bad, so having inflation above target is bad, but also important to remember having inflation below target is also bad and in this formulation it is equally bad to have either positive and negative gaps. Because the economy is going to be hit by shocks after you choose your level of accommodation, the monetary policymaker is going to choose the level of accommodation so as to minimize the expected loss averaging across all the shocks that could hit the economy.

So this average loss can be broken into two pieces. The first piece is the mean size of the gap squared, capturing how close you are on average to 0 in terms of the gap. Then the other piece is how much the gap wiggles, technically the variance of the gap. Both of those are bad: you don't want wiggles in the gap, and you'd like to be as close as possible to 0 on average. The typical assumption that we make when we think about formulating monetary policy is that the monetary policymaker can't influence the variance of the shocks. So that second piece is not really being influenced by monetary policy. Then minimizing expected loss amounts to getting the gap as close as possible to 0 on average. So the policymaker should choose a level of accommodation that minimizes, eliminates the gap on average. You're not going to be able to do that because there are shocks hitting you, so the realization might be above 0 or below 0 but on average you try to get it to 0. In my example, you try to get inflation equal to target on average by your choice of accommodation.

What about financial stability? How does that play into things? Well, the usual way we think about this is that a higher level of accommodation increases the risk of financial instability in addition to influencing the gap. So how does this show up? The risk of financial instability can mean that the higher level of accommodation can actually increase the wiggles in your gap. So this consideration does not affect your ability to necessarily eliminate the gap on average, but it's affecting the wiggles of the gap. So now your choice of accommodation is going to trade off the first piece versus the second piece. It's going to trade off how close you're getting to 0 on average versus the wiggles in the gap.

This trade-off means that you're generally going to be choosing a level of accommodation that results in an average gap which is less than 0. You're willing to give up a little bit of mean in other words in order to get less risk in X. You're willing to lower the level of accommodation or to avoid the wiggles that you otherwise get in X. This is not an interesting statement in and of itself though. The mean of X being less than 0 doesn't tell you how much less than 0 it is. It could be minus $-1*10^{50}$, which is a very small number.

So let's think about comparing two monetary policy alternatives. Let's label the first policy A* as the one that would set the gap equal to 0 on average. The only reason to pick another policy (A**) that less accommodative and leaves a gap that is less than 0 is if this second policy reduces variance by enough relative to A*. So wiggles under A** must be much lower than under A* to compensate for not making the gap 0.

This inequality summarizes, I think, the problem that we face. We know a lot about how to estimate the average gap given a choice of level of accommodation. My own view, as I have expressed publicly on a number of occasions, is that average gap remains large for the current choice of accommodation. But now with financial instability, if we are going to take that into account and try a different policy, we have to be able to figure out how to judge the progress on reducing wiggles. How do we assess the differences and the risks applied by different policy choices?

Now one simple, helpful simplification might be if you think about the following model of financial instability, that a crisis just causes the gap to fall by some big amount delta. You might think about inflation falling sharply or employment falling sharply. Then monetary accommodation changes the probability of that crisis. You can reduce the difference in the variances to be a difference in probabilities multiplied by the square of the impact of the crisis. So now we need to know the difference of the probabilities and the impact of the crisis on the gap. That's the basic framework. Once you take account of financial instability, monetary policy is about trading off mean versus variance, and it's no longer just about trying to get the gap as close as possible to 0. You're going to be willing to give that up, but now we have to get into a very different game as monetary policymakers of actually trying to assess the risk associated in a systemic way, the risk associated to our policy choices.

So how does the Monetary Policy Report fit into all this? I think there are some very important messages in the report, and it really makes you think about the need to think about residual systemic risk as a monetary policymaker because financial instability can rise from institutions that are non-banks, relatively unleveraged and solvent. I think another key message is asset flows contain key information about financial system risks. I think the good news for the public is that these ideas already do shape the Fed's surveillance of the financial system. We take a very broad look at the financial system, but these ideas that we shouldn't just be looking at banks, certainly a part of our thinking of what's going on in the financial system. The basic mechanism is an amplification mechanism whereby easy money leads to a low risk premium. Tight money leads to a high risk premium. This amplification mechanism means that seemingly small changes in the monetary policy stance can have big effects on financial market conditions. Now as somebody who likes accommodation, I have to say there's a positive associated to this in that actually our accommodative policies are really super stimulative which is a good thing. But they didn't emphasize that in their paper. Instead, the problem they emphasize is that seemingly small changes in the stance of monetary policy can have big effects on financial market conditions. I think the authors are persuasive that this was an element in the taper tantrum. The basic problem then for monetary policymakers is that easing policy now increased the later risk of possibly having a rapid tightening in financial market conditions. The basic thing is that eventually policy has to normalize and that normalization is going to include a retrace in the risk premia in their model. That means you can have a very rapid change in financial market conditions.

How should policymakers take that into account? Well I think the mean variance framework that I laid out earlier helps with that. The key question now which is outside the scope of this particular paper, but one you'd have to ask if you wanted to use it as a policymaker, is how does this increased financial market risk map into macroeconomic risks? How much does the variance of your gap, the the wiggles in your gap, increase because as increased risk of rapid tightening in financial market conditions. Maybe we can think about this in this lumpy way that I described. You just think about the probability of a rapid tightening and the impact of that has on your gap variables.

I certainly don't have the answers to those questions, but we do have a little information maybe about this from our 2013 experience. Financial market conditions did tighten very rapidly from May to August. Mortgage rates and 10-year yields rose by over 1 percentage point. Now arguably this large increase in yields only happened because the monetary policy of the time had lowered yields so much by say May 1st. But how did this rapid tightening of financial market conditions worsen economic outcomes? Was real GDP in 2013, the second half of 2013 that much lower? Now I want to be clear here. I'm not asking if the tightness of conditions of the second half of 2013 lowered economic performance. Presumably it did. That's how monetary policy works. My question is about the rapidity, the speed of retracing. How much did that contribute to a weaker performance in terms of the macroeconomy in the second half of 2013? I have my priors on that, which I don't think I see much evidence of an effect, but you know that's my priors. I do think that's the right way to try and push this paper in the next direction and try to make it useful for policy. So let me wrap up.

The mean variance framework that I describe implies that when you're confronting two policy choices, it's not enough to be able to just project what's going to happen to your relevant gap variable or to forecast the gap for your choice of accommodation as many central banks including the Fed focus upon doing. You also will need to be thinking about the differences and the variance of that gap, how much are the risks associated with the gap given your choice of accommodation, and maybe if you're just willing to focus on lumpy crises that could just have a sharp, sudden impact on your gap variable of interest, you might be able to simplify that problem by just looking at the difference of the probability of that crisis occurring multiplied by the square of the impact. Now I think a Monetary Policy Report suggests that these kinds of assessments are not going to be easy ones to make. We can't just look at the usual suspects. We have to take a broad kind of look at the financial system that we are trying to do with the Federal Reserve System. And the rate of change of financial market conditions and not just the level of financial market conditions could affect macroeconomic outcomes. As a PhD economist, the conclusions are the usual one; there is considerable need for ongoing research in this area, new theory and new empirics.

I will add one editorial point from my point of view, which is that we don't need this theory in empirics to be able to make decisions in March of 2014. I think the financial instability is something that I think we have to be thinking about, but I think the average gap remains sufficiently large. I can't think of it as being dwarfed by any kind of differences of variance as this point in time. So what does that mean? I think we have 2 to 3 years to be thinking about this problem and then getting it right. Thank you very much.

COMMENTS

By Jeremy C. Stein

BOARD OF GOVERNORS OF THE FEDERAL RESERVE BANK SYSTEM

I am delighted to have the opportunity to discuss the paper "Market Tantrums and Monetary Policy." It is timely, provocative, and extremely insightful. Let me start by summarizing what I take to be the paper's main messages.[1] First, the authors argue that policymakers should pay careful attention not just to measures of leverage in the banking and shadow banking sectors, but also to the financial stability risks that might arise from the behavior of unlevered asset managers, such as those running various types of bond funds. Notably, assets under management in fixed-income funds have grown dramatically in the years since the onset of the financial crisis, even while various measures of financial-sector leverage have either continued to decline or remained subdued.

Second, the authors develop a model of agency problems in delegated asset management, according to which an environment of low short-term rates can encourage asset managers concerned with their relative performance rankings to "reach for yield," which in turn acts to compress risk premiums. Moreover, the model has the feature that this reach for yield can end badly, with a sudden and sharp correction in risk premiums that arises endogenously in response to a small tightening of monetary policy. The events of the spring and summer of 2013, when there was a rapid rise in bond market term premiums, are cited as a leading example of what the model sets out to capture.

---

1.   The views expressed here are my own and are not necessarily shared by other members of the Federal Reserve Board and the Federal Open Market Committee. I am grateful to Nellie Liang for helpful conversations.

Third, the authors assert that the conventional regulatory toolkit, which is largely designed to contain intermediary leverage, is not well suited to dealing with the asset-management sector. Given this limitation of regulation, and because monetary policy has a direct influence on the behavior of asset managers, the financial stability risks that these managers create should be factored into the design and conduct of monetary policy. Presumably, this consideration would imply that monetary policy should be somewhat less easy in a weak economy, all else being equal, to reduce the probability of an undesirable upward spike in rates and credit spreads down the road. The authors are careful to note that "our analysis neither invalidates nor validates the course the Federal Reserve has actually taken."[2] Rather, they are highlighting a set of considerations that they believe should ultimately be incorporated into the design of a monetary policy framework. This is the spirit in which I will discuss the paper--not as a comment on the current stance of policy, but as an exploration of the factors that should be taken into account when thinking about the tradeoffs associated with monetary policy more generally.

The model in the paper is a simple one, and it does a nice job of framing the issues. In particular, here is how I think about the value-added of the theory: On the one hand, an emerging body of empirical work documents that an easing of monetary policy--even via conventional policy tools in normal times--tends to reduce both the term premiums on long-term Treasury bonds and the credit spreads on corporate bonds.[3] That is, monetary policy tends to work in part through its effect on capital market risk premiums, perhaps through some sort of risk-taking or reaching-for-yield mechanism.

On the other hand, while this empirical observation sheds some interesting light on *how* monetary policy influences the real economy, it does not by itself suggest that there is any financial stability dark side to the lowered risk premiums that go with monetary accommodation. For there to be any meaningful tradeoff, there would have to be some sort of asymmetry in the unwinding of these risk premiums, whereby the eventual reversal either happens more abruptly, or causes larger economic effects, than the initial compression. Said a little differently, if an easing of Federal Reserve policy puts downward pressure on term premiums and credit spreads, and if this downward pressure is only gradually reversed as policy begins to tighten, then what is the problem?

The nice feature of the model is that it speaks to this asymmetry. That is, it features a gradual compression of risk spreads during a period of monetary ease, and then, when policy begins to tighten, it delivers a sharp and abrupt correction, driven by a particular form of market dynamics.

---

2.   See Feroli and others (2014), p. 6.

3.   See, for example, Hanson and Stein (2012); Gertler and Karadi (2013); and Gilchrist, Lopez-Salido, and Zakrajsek (2013).

Of course, this is just a theoretical prediction. One thing that the paper does not do, but which would be very helpful in assessing the real-world relevance of the model, would be to see if this sort of asymmetry in bond returns is present in the data. In particular, if I am interpreting the model correctly, it implies a specific form of conditional volatility and skewness in bond returns. For example, when term premiums are unusually low relative to historical norms, the model suggests an elevated probability of a sharp upward spike in rates. I don't know of any evidence that bears on this hypothesis in the bond market, though an analogous pattern does appear in stock market returns.[4]

It is worth saying a little about the "musical chairs" mechanism that leads to the sharp spike in rates. The fund managers in the model care about their relative performance in that they are averse to posting lower returns than their peers, holding fixed absolute performance. These relative-performance concerns induce a form of strategic complementarity of fund manager actions. Specifically, as short-term rates begin to rise and fund manager i contemplates whether she should bail out of long-term bonds and move into short-term bills, she is more apt to do so if she thinks that some other manager, j, is also going to bail--because she is worried that otherwise, she may wind up underperforming manager j and finishing last in the relative-performance tournament.

While appearing in a different guise here, this strategic-complementarity effect-- the idea that any one agent is in more of a rush to get out when he or she thinks that others may also want to get out--is essentially the same mechanism that drives bank runs in the classic work of Diamond and Dybvig, and that, in one manifestation or another, creates financial fragility in many other settings.[5] However, one thing that is distinctive about the variant presented in the current paper is that there is a clear prediction of exactly what sets off the run for the exits on the part of money managers--namely, a small increase in short rates beyond a certain threshold level.[6]

The model focuses on one particular source of run-like fragility that might emanate from the asset-management sector, but there are others. One that the paper briefly mentions, and that is worth a fuller treatment, has to do with the potential for outflows of assets under management (AUM) from open-end funds. Note that

---

4.   See Chen, Hong, and Stein (2001). They document that, consistent with a "bubble popping" view, stock returns are more negatively skewed when past returns have been positive and when valuation ratios (for example, market-to-book ratios) are high. Alternatively, the ratio of downside to upside volatility is unusually high in such circumstances.

5.   See Diamond and Dybvig (1983).

6.   This feature is in contrast to many other models in the Diamond-Dybvig (1983) tradition, which have multiple equilibria and hence convey a sense of fragility, but have less to say about what underlying variable tips the scales toward a run-like equilibrium. The more pinned-down nature of the model in this paper comes from an application of the global-games methodology described in Morris and Shin (2003).

the model is effectively one of a closed-end fund, since the manager is assumed to have a fixed amount of AUM; the fragility, in this case, comes entirely from the manager's portfolio allocation decision and from the strategic interaction among *fund managers*. But another source of run-like risk comes from the strategic interaction among *fund investors* and the incentives that each of them may have to get out before others do when asset values are at risk of declining.

These AUM-driven run dynamics are more likely to arise in those open-end funds that hold relatively illiquid assets. The key question in determining whether there is a strategic complementarity in the withdrawal decisions of fund investors is, When investor i exits on day t, does the net asset value (NAV) at the end of the day that defines investor i's exit price fully reflect the ultimate price effect of the sales created by his exit? If not, those investors who stay behind are hurt, which is what creates run incentives. And, if the run incentives are strong enough, then a credit-oriented bond fund starts looking pretty bank-like. The fact that its liabilities are not technically debt claims is not all that helpful in this case--they are still demandable, and hence investors can pull out very rapidly if the terms of exit create a penalty for being last out the door.

A fund's stated NAV is less likely to keep pace with the ultimate price impact of investor withdrawals if the underlying assets are illiquid, for two distinct reasons. First, some of the assets are likely to have stale prices--that is, not to have been recently marked to market. And, second, if most of a fund's assets are illiquid securities, its manager will be inclined to accommodate early exits by drawing down on the fund's cash reserve while planning to sell securities and replenish the cash stock later.

Why, at the end of the day, should one care if run-like incentives come predominantly from the strategic behavior of fund investors, as opposed to that of fund managers? Isn't there the same worrisome fragility in either case? Perhaps, but the policy response may differ depending on the exact diagnosis. In the former case, when the primary worry is AUM runs on the part of investors, there is at least in principle a natural regulatory fix: One could impose exit fees on open-end funds that are related to the illiquidity of the funds' assets, in an effort to make departing investors more fully internalize the costs that they impose on those who stay behind. In the latter case, when the problem is driven more by the portfolio choices of fund managers, it is harder for me to see an obvious regulatory response, so I am more inclined to share the authors' view that if there is, indeed, a significant financial stability problem, monetary policy would be left to take up some of the slack.

To be clear, I am not advocating for exit fees of the sort I just described; I do not think we know enough about the empirical relevance of the AUM-run mechanism, to say nothing of its quantitative importance, to be making such recommendations at this point. But, given the detailed nature of the microdata that are available on individual fund holdings and returns, there is clearly room to make significant further progress on this front. Indeed, recent work by Chen, Goldstein, and Jiang is very much in this spirit, although it restricts its analysis to equity funds and doesn't consider the fixed-income categories that are the focus of the current paper.[7]

With this framing in mind, let me comment briefly on the empirical work in the paper. There is a lot of it, and I will just touch on a couple of points. A first observation is that the heavy focus on flows in and out of funds is a bit at odds with the theoretical model. As I mentioned earlier, the model, taken literally, is one of closed-end funds with fixed AUM. If one were interested in testing the specific mechanism in the model most directly, it seems to me that one would want to look not at fund flows but rather at the *portfolio allocations* within each fund. For example, the model suggests that, during the unfolding of an episode of bond market volatility like the one in the spring and summer of last year, we should see a coordinated shift among bond managers out of long-term bonds and into bills so that the average durations of their portfolios would co-move strongly together. There is a well-developed empirical literature on herding among fund managers in their portfolio allocations, but, as far as I know, this work has not looked at how such herding responds to changes in the monetary policy environment.[8] So this avenue seems like a potentially promising one to pursue.

The paper's focus on flows in and out of funds is, however, well suited to thinking about mechanisms related to AUM-run dynamics. In this regard, a particularly interesting set of findings has to do with the ability of flows to forecast future asset returns, even controlling for past returns. And, most notably, this forecasting effect is much stronger in the less liquid high-yield and emerging market categories than it is in U.S. Treasury securities; indeed, it is essentially nonexistent in the latter category. While not a decisive test, this pattern is consistent with one of the necessary preconditions for the existence of strategic complementarities and run-like dynamics. Again, the key idea is that, when a fund's assets are illiquid, outflows today are met in part with drawdowns from cash reserves, with the other assets being sold off more gradually over time--hence, the predictable downward pressure on prices going forward. This predictability is what creates the incentive for any given investor to pull out quickly if he or she sees a large number of co-investors pulling out.[9]

Let me summarize by noting the areas in which I agree most closely with the authors and by adding one key qualification. First, I think they are absolutely on target in emphasizing that the rapid growth of fixed-income funds--as well as other, similar vehicles--bears careful watching. As they point out, it would be a mistake to be complacent about this phenomenon simply because such funds are unlevered.

---

7.   See Chen, Goldstein, and Jiang (2010).

8.   Chevalier and Ellison (1999) is a classic reference.

9.   Indeed, the results in the paper closely parallel those in Chen, Goldstein, and Jiang (2010), who find that fund flows forecast future returns more strongly among those equity funds that hold relatively illiquid stocks

Other economic mechanisms can mimic the run-like incentives associated with short-term debt financing, and one or more of these mechanisms may well be present in fixed-income funds.

Second, I also agree that there is no general separation principle for monetary policy and financial stability. Monetary policy is fundamentally in the business of altering risk premiums such as term premiums and credit spreads. So monetary policymakers cannot wash their hands of what happens when these spreads revert sharply. If these abrupt reversions also turn out to have nontrivial economic consequences, then they are clearly of potential relevance to policymakers.

My one qualification is as follows: In the absence of a general separation principle, when one might consider addressing financial stability issues either with regulation or with monetary policy, it becomes all the more critical to get the case-by-case analysis right--that is, to really dig into the microeconomic details of the presumed market failure and to ask when a regulatory intervention is comparatively more efficient than a monetary one, or vice versa. So while I think it is important to remain heterodox and to be open to taking either approach, I would not want to rule out the possibility that some of the risks identified by the authors could be mitigated, at least in part, via a regulatory approach. I look forward to seeing more work that helps us sort through these challenging issues.

References

Chen, Joseph, Harrison Hong, and Jeremy C. Stein (2001). "Forecasting Crashes: Trading Volume, Past Returns, and Conditional Skewness in Stock Prices," *Journal of Financial Economics,* vol. 61, pp. 345-81, www.princeton.edu/~hhong/jfe-forcrash.pdf.

Chen, Qi, Itay Goldstein, and Wei Jiang (2010). "Payoff Complementarities and Financial Fragility: Evidence from Mutual Fund Outflows," *Journal of Financial Economics,* vol. 97 (2), pp. 239-62.

Chevalier, Judith, and Glenn Ellison (1999). "Career Concerns of Mutual Fund Managers," *Quarterly Journal of Economics,* vol. 114 (2), pp. 389-432.

Diamond, Douglas, and Philip Dybvig (1983). "Bank Runs, Deposit Insurance, and Liquidity," *Journal of Political Economy,* vol. 91, pp. 401-19.

Feroli, Michael, Anil K. Kashyap, Kermit Schoenholtz, and Hyun Song Shin (2014). "Market Tantrums and Monetary Policy," paper presented at the 2014 U.S. Monetary Policy Forum, New York, February 28.

(for example, small-cap stocks). Moreover, Chen, Goldstein, and Jiang cast their regressions as being an explicit test of the strategic-complementarity hypothesis.

Gertler, Mark, and Peter Karadi (2013). "Monetary Policy Surprises, Credit Costs and Economic Activity," working paper, October, www.econ.nyu.edu/user/gertlerm/GertlerKaradi2013Oct3draftd-3.pdf.

Gilchrist, Simon, David Lopez-Salido, and Egon Zakrajsek (2013). "Monetary Policy and Real Borrowing Costs at the Zero Lower Bound," Finance and Economics Discussion Series 2014-03. Washington: Board of Governors of the Federal Reserve System, December, available at www.federalreserve.gov/pubs/feds/2014/201403/201403abs.html.

Hanson, Samuel, and Jeremy C. Stein (2012). "Monetary Policy and Long-Term Real Rates," Finance and Economics Discussion Series 2012-46. Washington: Board of Governors of the Federal Reserve System, July, available at www.federalreserve.gov/pubs/feds/2012/index.html.

Morris, Stephen, and Hyun Song Shin (2003). "Global Games: Theory and Applications," in Mathias Dewatripont, Lars Peter Hansen, and Stephen J. Turnovsky, eds., *Advances in Economics and Econometrics: Theory and Applications: Eighth World Congress,* vol. 1. New York: Cambridge University Press, pp. 56-114.

U.S. Monetary Policy Forum 2014

KEYNOTE SPEECH

By Robert E. Rubin

COUNCIL ON FOREIGN RELATIONS

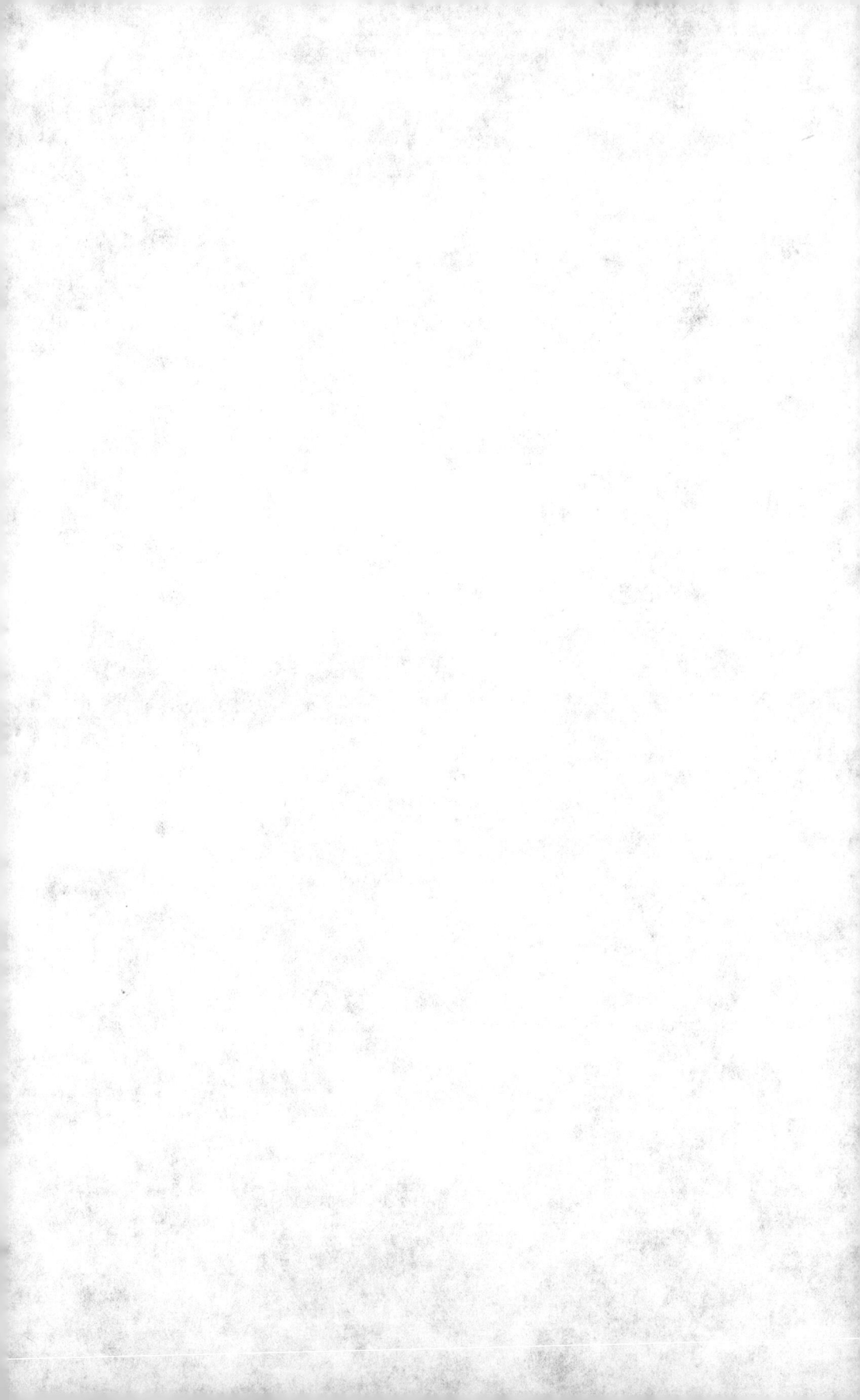

At this assemblage of distinguished economists, I was asked to discuss the views I developed as a practitioner, especially during the 26 years that I had responsibility for some and then all of Goldman Sachs' trading and arbitrage activities, and then during my time in government.

In a few moments, I will turn to my outlook for 2014. My purpose is not to be an economic forecaster – though my view differs somewhat from what is becoming the prevailing view. But, rather this discussion provides a lens for focusing on approaches to gauging the economic outlook, market behavior, and the effects of policy. I will also discuss fiscal and monetary policy themselves.

My perspective, as developed over many years, is that judgments on all these matters should draw on experience with a wide range of relevant variables, including market and business psychology and confidence, economic policy, politics and government functionality, tail risks, and much else.

Models can help inform decisions. But my experience suggests that models don't begin to capture the complexities of reality. Otherwise, every private and public sector institution that could afford sophisticated models and highly-capable analysts would have a high level of accuracy in predicting the future and the effects of policy. And, that's certainly not the case.

Forecasting models, as I understand them, assume that market participants and business decision-makers rationally respond to the factors in the model, and that, in a broad sense, past relationships or other data, can be relied on in projecting the future. My experience, however, suggests that market and business behavior reflects a wide range of factors and their uncertainties that go way beyond what models capture, including, critically, emotions, the psychology of business and markets, and the vagaries of politics and finance. Obviously, models can be adjusted to reflect assumptions about psychology, political decisions about policy, and much else. But that raises the question of how realistic and robust are those assumptions are, and what the uncertainties around them may be.

As a consequence of all this, I believe that while models can usefully inform decisions, effective decision-making for investment, business and policy requires shrewd and experienced judgment. Prediction is always highly uncertain, but in our own trading at Goldman, I concluded that some people had a special ability here and provided real value added.

A related point is that the causes of short-term market behavior are often uncertain, even *ex post*. Frequently, the asserted cause is a proximate factor, but the real cause is underlying excess that sooner or later would have resulted in a market reaction.

One more observation here is that because of the emotional and psychological factors that affect market behavior, I think markets in the short-run are often inefficient – a growing view as you know – in the sense that they don't rationally reflect long-run fundamentals.

The psychology of markets was exemplified on Monday, October 19, 1987. The Dow Jones declined 22% even though no notable event occurred between Friday of the prior week and Monday. Similarly, NASDAQ went to a high of over 5,000 in the year 2000, based largely on technology stocks, and a year later it was at 2,250. Fischer Black, whom I got to know well when he was at Goldman Sachs, wrote a famous article called "Noise" after some years at the firm. The article reflected his changing views about the efficiency of markets, and the discussions he and I and others at Goldman Sachs had often had. By implication, the article also suggested the uncertainties around prediction and the limits of economic models.

In any case, no matter how you approach decision-making, as you well know, all issues that matter are complex, all decisions are about probabilities, and all conclusions about those probabilities, whether by models or human judgment, are themselves inherently uncertain. And, for me, that uncertainty itself is a significant factor in decisionmaking, whether about investments or policy.

This point about probabilities is obvious, but as Stan Fischer once said to me, while anyone who is thoughtful will recognize the probabilistic nature of decision-making, few internalize it and operate that way.

At Goldman Sachs, I frequently overruled traders and arbitrageurs who, on the one hand, thought of themselves as probabilistic, but on the other hand, acted on conviction without adequately taking into account the probabilities of a negative outcome. At Treasury, we thought in terms of probability distributions, but Washington's approach to decision-making tends to be more black and white.

Now, having discussed my larger point about decision-making, especially in an uncertain world, let me turn to the short-term economic outlook.

Many thoughtful analysts have increased their growth estimates for 2014 to the neighborhood of 3% or more, based largely on a substantial reduction of fiscal drag compared to 2013. And that may turn out to be the best judgment about the central case.

However, if you look at the components of demand, the numbers as they currently stand, if extrapolated out, would produce a somewhat slower rate of growth. That's true on a year-over-year basis, or even on a 4th quarter over 4th quarter basis, when adjusted for the substantial decline in 4th quarter inflation and its effect on increasing average real wages. The question with respect to the more affirmative forecasts is where will the impetus come from to make these better forecasts materialize?

Consider consumption, which, as we all know, is by far the largest component of GDP, and is driven predominately by labor income.

Looking at labor income, job growth of 200,000 jobs a month, which is well in excess of last year's rate, provides an increase of only 1.7% per year. The reduction in public sector jobs last year was very small, so taking that reduction out of last year's numbers doesn't affect the result. The other two components of labor income are average real wages, which are roughly stagnant, except in the last quarter due to the reduction in inflation, and hours worked, which are up modestly. Put this all together, and labor income would grow relatively slowly.

There could be a wealth effect from the enormous increase in stock prices and the increase in housing prices, but that would likely be small, given the distribution of the gains and the limited potential for the savings rate to fall.

The large reduction in fiscal drag eliminates a negative, but that still leaves the question of the impetus for significant improvement. Most analysts who project stronger growth focus on a revival of business investment as the variable that will break us out of this sluggish mode and set off a virtuous cycle. However, business investment, while somewhat better recently, has been basically sluggish.

Anecdotal evidence suggests sluggish investment will probably continue. I recently hosted a dinner for a group of ten directors of major American companies, and not a single one expected either strong growth in business investment or strong growth in the economy for 2014. Some analysts play down the value of anecdotal evidence in favor of quantitative analysis, and Keynes referred dismissively to those who think "their nose is a nobler organ than their brain." I am no Keynes, but everything I have seen suggests using both seriously in making decisions.

My conclusion is that growth is likely to remain sluggish this year and, unless government becomes functional again, is quite likely to remain sluggish for an extended time. Even if the more promising projections seem more persuasive, that would still be a slow recovery by historical standards, and with substantial uncertainties.

There is also the question of tail risks. Over a one-year period, geopolitical developments, Eurozone and emerging market destabilization, and momentous, unanticipated developments are hopefully low probabilities. But they are realistic possibilities, with huge consequences. None of these risks seem to be reflected in markets, except, perhaps, sporadically or in forecasting models.

To make this even more complex, a tail risk for any given year may have a material probability of materializing at some point over a longer period. Furthermore, there are overarching risks of immense potential impact that don't fall into time slots, like global warming and the long-term economic consequences of wage stagnation, income inequality, and long-term unemployment.

Tail risks, and the longer-term analogues to tail risks, pose a question with no good answer, which is, how should investors and policymakers deal with these risks? Ignoring them can severely or even catastrophically affect you. But protecting yourself sufficiently to avoid serious damage may cost you the opportunities of the far more likely scenarios. My best answer has been to recognize these risks, and modulate in some ways to reduce—though not eliminate—exposure.

I do think policy could provide the impetus for breaking out of our sluggish or, at best, slow recovery. In this context, the debate about jobs and growth now, versus fiscal discipline for the longer term, poses a false choice that diverts focus from what should be done. A well-constructed fiscal program could generate growth, jobs and investment now, by replacing the current fiscal drag with positive government demand and, importantly, by increasing business confidence.

Confidence is key to business and consumer decisions and economic conditions more generally, and I think confidence is key to breaking out of our slow recovery. Keynes made the point about when he coined the phrase, "animal spirits" in the "The General Theory." And, he expressed that same idea, though somewhat differently, in his famous 1938 letter to FDR. And, the Clinton Administration's 1993 deficit reduction program's contribution to growth was materially a product of improved confidence. A sound fiscal program could increase business confidence significantly both by reducing policy uncertainty and by reducing the enormous concern about government dysfunction – views I hear frequently from business people. At the same time, this program could contribute to meeting the imperative for sound fiscal conditions for the next decade and the decades beyond.

That fiscal program would be comprised of at least four components. First, rescission of the sequester, which has already been reduced slightly in the recent budget agreement. Second, fiscal discipline enacted now, but with implementation deferred for some specified period of time supported by a Senate Point of Order. Third, structural reform that increases revenues and puts entitlements on a sustainable path going forward financially. Our short-term fiscal position has improved, in part, because of what seems to be a structural decline in the rate of increase in healthcare costs. But, further structural reform would help address the market increases in the debt/GDP ratio later in the current budget window and serious increases in the decades beyond. It is also important to remember that we have already surrendered the resilience that our strong fiscal position at the beginning of the last decade gave us, that could have enabled us to deal far more effectively with the financial crisis, and even prior to the fiscal crisis, our debt/GDP position was almost half of what it is today – which again affects resilience going forward. Further structural measures would also and very importantly free up funds for critically-needed public investment, like infrastructure, basic research, and so much else. Structural measures like this are especially germane in promoting business confidence relevant to investment decisions, because those decisions often have time horizons of five, ten, or more years. Fourth, this program would provide the sound fiscal context for a significant upfront stimulus.

A stand-alone stimulus is a more complex matter. It might lead to a high multiple, ongoing growth, and a virtuous cycle. But it may also peter out, ending up without sustained growth and a worsened debt-to-GDP ratio. Interest rates probably wouldn't react significantly, given current conditions, though they might. The key issue is confidence. The immediate demand could be a substantial boost to confidence that could then provide the impetus for breaking out of our sluggish growth. But enacting stimulus without fiscal discipline, and the increase in debt-to-GDP, could negatively affect confidence, by increasing uncertainty about future policy and concern about government functionality. Thus, I believe enacting stimulus in the context of a broader program of fiscal discipline would be preferable to a stand-alone stimulus.

Measures in other areas could also provide substantive benefit now and improve confidence—for example, immigration reform, trade, and regulation that provides strong protection, but also weighs costs and benefits.

All of these issues are substantively and politically complex – especially with the need to meet the multiple imperatives of growth, widespread income gains and sharing in the benefits of growth and economic security. But I believe our legislative challenges could be effectively addressed by negotiators who had very different views, but also had a willingness to engage in principled compromise. However, we are in a state of near gridlock. Recent actions by Congress—one to raise the debt ceiling without conditions; the other, a budget agreement that averted a government shutdown—were considered by some to indicate that conditions are improving in Washington. I had exactly the opposite reaction. Characterizing these actions as evidence that our system can work shows just how broken the system really is.

Having said all that, I think the probability is high that our system will return to the functionality necessary to meet our challenges, though the process may be lengthy and messy. Our political system has a history of resilience; we have a dynamic culture; and politics change rapidly in America. At any rate, whatever happens to our system's functionality, political decision-making is central to market and economic outcomes.

Thus, policymakers, including central banks, should incorporate political analysis as a key element in gauging future conditions and in making policy judgments.

Another major influence on economic conditions over the next year and in the years ahead will be the effects of QE3. This is complicated and controversial and will probably be studied and debated for a long time as a guide to future central bank actions. I'm just going to make a few comments.

The first program of quantitative easing was a courageous and effective response to the acute phase of the financial crisis. Some say QE3 was warranted by high unemployment and the absence of other policy due to government dysfunction. Clearly, our high unemployment, the number of discouraged works, long-term unemployment and stagnant median real wages are vital economic issues. The right criterion for action, however, is not the absence of alternatives, but the balance of risks and rewards.

There are widely-held questions about the benefits of QE3. But the risks seem to me real, and at least threefold. Firstly, QE3 created a comfort about rates, in-dependent of whatever the actual effects may have been, that put less pressure on politicians to act. Secondly, financial moral hazard, where again even if the actual effect on bond markets was small, that same comfort may have heightened the tendency to reach for yield further out on the risk curve, increasing the likelihood of excesses and subsequent destabilization. Thirdly, and most concerning to me is the possible economic and market effects of unwinding the Fed's vast increase in its balance sheet from under $1.0 trillion to $4.0 trillion now, and the commensurate increase in liquidity, however that unwinding is accomplished.

Monetary policy decisions always involve large uncertainties. And those uncer-tainties may be heightened with such great increases.

Calibrating tapering, when to start tightening, and managing the pace and mag-nitude of tightening requires judgments about the behavior and psychology of creditors, borrowers, businesses, consumers and financial markets in unprecedented circumstances. And all of those reactions are unpredictable.

In financial circles, the greater concern is about navigating these unchartered wa-ters about inflation. But my view is that there is at least an equal chance monetary action could push the economy into a downturn.

There is a perspective that these risks can be avoided by holding bonds until maturity, and tightening by increasing interest rates on excess reserves. But, it seems to me that there is no magic wand. Vast increases in liquidity have been created that banks have not lent out but instead deposited with the Fed as excess reserves.

When credit demand picks up substantially, however far in the future that may be, banks can draw the reserves down at will to extend credit. The increased capital requirements involved would prevent lending, but would be part of a bank's rele-vant risk/return calculation. And, again, there is no way to reliably predict the be-havior of creditors, borrowers, lenders and markets in this unprecedented situation. Thus, nobody knows how much rates would have to be increased to accomplish the desired tightening, what the effects might be and how volatile the situation might become. And, it seems to me the other technical suggestions that have been discussed have similar problems.

Only time will tell how the unwinding of QE3 works out, and efforts to gauge those consequences involve factors and uncertainties way beyond the ambit of current economic models.

Many analysts say the unwinding is highly likely to be relatively benign; others are more concerned. More broadly, questions about the positive and negative effects of QE3 will remain highly uncertain, both for prediction now and for evaluation *ex post*. (Many forces act on markets and economic behavior, and reliably measuring their relative causal weight is impossible.)

(This is alternative language for starting this topic: As to forward guidance, let me just say that the reliance on it by investors, or commitment to it by central banks, seem to me to raise interesting questions in light of the impossibility of predicting with confidence what conditions will be in six months or more in the future.)

I'll raise one final question on monetary policy, which is how forward guidance will be seen by market participants over time. No one can predict with a high level of confidence what conditions will be six months or more in the future. Thus, forward guidance, even with conditionality, could become counterproductive over the period involved, and presumably subject to change. Conversely, inflexible commitment to forward guidance would seem unwise.

Let me end on a positive note. For the long term, I would rather invest in the United States than in any other economy. Our country has enormous absolute and comparative strengths. The key to realizing that potential is sound and effective policy. And that takes us back to two main themes of these remarks. One, deciding how to approach the complexities and uncertainties that pervade policy decision-making. And two, all the good policy thinking in the world doesn't matter unless the politics works. Thus, in the final analysis, the fundamental challenge upon which our future depends is effective governance. And, despite today's discouraging dysfunction, I believe we are highly likely to restore a reasonable level of government functionality. Thank you.

U.S. Monetary Policy Forum 2014

Like It or Not, 90 Percent of a 'Successful Fed Communications' Strategy Comes from Simply Pursuing a Goal-oriented Monetary Policy Strategy

Charles L. Evans

PRESIDENT AND CHIEF EXECUTIVE OFFICER
FEDERAL RESERVE BANK OF CHICAGO

Thank you for inviting me to speak today about monetary policy strategy and communications. Before I begin my comments, let me note that the views I express here are my own and do not necessarily reflect the views of the Federal Reserve Bank of Chicago or of my colleagues on the Federal Open Market Committee (FOMC) or within the Federal Reserve System.

Communications are critical for effective monetary policy strategy – they are inextricably linked. There are different approaches to, and much debate regarding, best practices.

One approach is to have a full-throated discussion at the FOMC meetings, release a statement summarizing our view and then have the Chair hold a quarterly press conference to announce and explain the policy action to the public. This approach also includes describing how the action is intended to achieve the Committee's policy goals. These post-meeting communications are followed by the release of the minutes, which give a fuller description of the comments made at the meeting. An alternative approach is to adopt a simple policy rule, like Taylor's 1993 policy rule. The Committee would follow the policy rule prescription and report on any particular details regarding how the rule was implemented at each meeting. Again, a press conference could be used as a communications enhancement.

Although all central banks face these strategy and communications issues, and they implement them somewhat differently, my view is that 90 percent of the communications challenge is met by expressing policy intentions clearly so that the public can understand the Federal Reserve's goals and how the Fed is committed to achieving these goals in a timely fashion (Slide 1). A clear expression of policy intentions requires stating the Fed's policy goals clearly and explicitly. These messages need to be repeated – over and over again. It is also necessary to clearly demonstrate our commitment to achieving these goals in a timely fashion with policyactions.

An equivalent and more operational statement of this principle is that the Fed should follow a goal-oriented monetary policy strategy and should provide full accountability (Slide 2). Notice the links between these two statements (Slide 3): "Express policy intentions clearly so that the public can understand the Federal Reserve's goals" is captured by "follow a goal-oriented monetary policy strategy." "The Fed's commitment to achieving these goals in a timely fashion" is captured by "provide full accountability." The final 10 percent of communications represents details that are crucially important for individuals and market participants, but the first 90 percent is the key to the public's understanding of ourpolicies.

Monetary Policy Strategy and Communications

- Express policy intentions clearly so that the public can understand the Federal Reserve's goals and demonstrate the Fed's commitment to achieving these goals in a timely fashion

Slide 1

Monetary Policy Strategy and Communications

- Express policy intentions clearly so that the public can understand the Federal Reserve's goals and demonstrate the Fed's commitment to achieving these goals in a timely fashion

- Follow a goal-oriented monetary policy strategy and provide full accountability

Slide 2

Monetary Policy Strategy and Communications

- Express policy intentions clearly so that the public can understand the Federal Reserve's goals and

demonstrate the Fed's commitment to achieving these goals in a timely fashion

- Follow a goal-oriented monetary policy strategy and

provide full accountability

Slide 3

The January 2012 statement of long-run monetary policy strategy clearly expresses the FOMC's policy intentions (Slide 4): It states that the FOMC's explicit inflation objective is 2 percent for the price index for personal consumption expenditures (PCE) in the long run and that maximum employment is associated with a sustainable unemployment rate that properly reflects structural developments that may alter this rate over time. Our long-run strategy also points to the Committee's Summary of Economic Projections (SEP) to provide a range of values for the sustainable unemployment rate. Currently, the central tendency for this range is between 5¼ percent and 5¾ percent. Finally, our strategy states that the Committee will use a balanced approach to reduce deviations from our long-run objectives.

Long-Run Strategy for Monetary Policy
(January 2012, reaffirmed thereafter every January)

- $\pi^* = 2\%$ PCE inflation

- $U_t^* \sim 5.2\% - 5.8\%$ time-varying
  Central tendency of SEP longer-run normal rate

- **Balanced approach** to reducing deviations of inflation
  and employment from long-run objectives

Slide 4

This balanced approach implies strongly that our policy loss function can provide what I refer to as "bull's-eye" accountability (slide 5). This entire chart is like a simple "corporate scorecard" for our two-dimensional policy objectives in unemployment and inflation outcomes. The circles provide collections of unemployment and inflation rates that are equally uncomfortable for FOMC participants. The chart clearly depicts the unemployment dilemma that the Committee still faced as of September 2011. For example, it tells us how a 9 percent unemployment rate can be depicted in "inflation- loss equivalent units" by showing what inflation rate gives an equivalent loss when unemployment is at its sustainable rate. The answer is 5½ percent inflation! All post- Volcker central bankers would respond to 5½ percent inflation as if their "hair was on fire." Such a situation would call for strong and decisive monetary action. The bull's-eye scorecard provides accountability. And indeed, in response to this loss, the FOMC acted. The FOMC had already employed QE2 in the fall of 2010. In August 2011, the FOMC employed a form of forward guidance and followed that up in September 2011 with the Maturity Extension Program, or "Operation Twist."

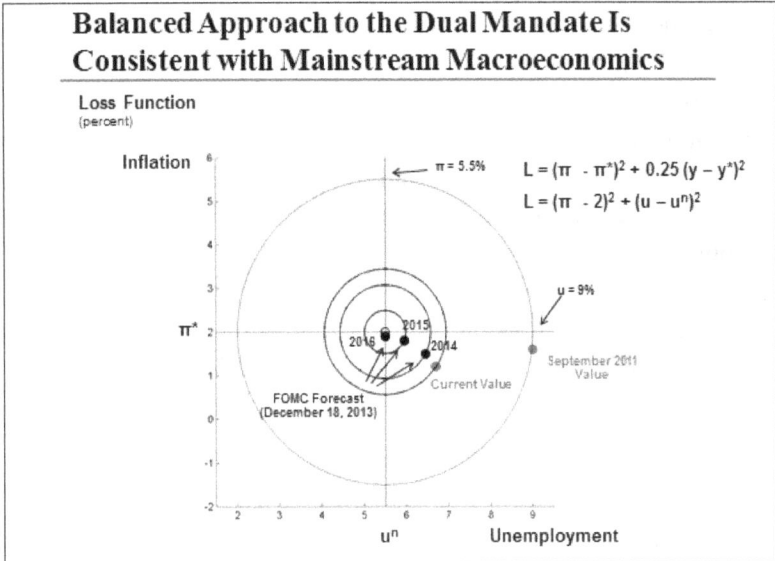

Balanced Approach to the Dual Mandate Is Consistent with Mainstream Macroeconomics

Loss Function (percent)

$L = (\pi - \pi^*)^2 + 0.25\,(y - y^*)^2$

$L = (\pi - 2)^2 + (u - u^n)^2$

Slide 5

The most recent December 2013 Summary of Economic Projections shows that the Committee forecasts that unemployment and inflation will reach the bull's-eye mark by the fourth quarter of 2016. This is a relatively slow attainment of our long-run goals. It also should be pointed out that these are still just projections of improvement, yet to be achieved. Nevertheless, the enhancements to our communications in recent years go a long way toward meeting our communications objectives by using this scorecard to depict progress toward our dual mandate goals.

Our actions are strongly reinforced when the public knows that the FOMC is committed to achieving the bull's-eye within a reasonable period of time with appropriate monetary policy actions. This is particularly true for unconventional policy actions. For example, consider Chairman Bernanke's April 2012 press conference. At this event, numerous questions from journalists expressed skepticism that the FOMC's Summary of Economic Projections indicated a clear commitment to closing the unemployment gap in a timely fashion. Following the adoption of our January 2012 strategy document, this public questioning was trying to assess whether these forecasts reflected a difference of opinion between the FOMC and the public on what is a "balanced approach to reducing imbalances," or whether the forecast reflected the difficult and time-consuming process of consensus policy decision-making. In either case, the open public discussion of the issue enhanced the Fed's accountability regarding the bull's-eye scorecard. The entire discussion was taking place in public and contemporaneously with the policy decision.

This is goal-oriented monetary policy with accountability. It is the combination of our January 2012 strategy statement, the quarterly SEP, the Chair's press conference and repetition.

So, my claim is that to be any good, monetary policy communications regarding policy actions must be consistent with the Fed expressing policy intentions clearly, so that the public can understand the Fed's goals and its commitment to achieving these goals in a timely fashion. This should be a principle for all effective monetary policy strategies and communications: to state monetary policy intentions clearly.

I will now be critical of incomplete attempts to solve this strategy and communications challenge by invoking and following an overly simple policy rule. John Taylor has repeatedly argued that the Fed has failed because it has not followed the 1993 Taylor rule. In March 2011, during his Senate testimony, Chairman Bernanke was asked why the Fed had not followed the Taylor rule.[1] Chairman Bernanke replied that Fed policy has been remarkably consistent with the 1999 version of the Taylor rule. He also pointed out several issues associated with the fact that there is a zero lower bound on the fed funds rate.

For me, there is a problem with simplistic approaches. Simple Taylor rules fail the strategic principle to express policy intentions clearly. At the zero lower bound, simple rules simply cannot be implemented. Accordingly, they cannot express policy intentions and do not allow the public to clearly understand the Fed goals and the Fed's commitment to achieving these goals in a timely fashion. During quieter, normal times when short-term interest rates are 2 percent or more, many approaches may work. But how structurally sound are these simple rules? If a policy rule is sturdy, the test of its structural foundation comes when a hurricane or an earthquake hits.

The 1999 Taylor rule captures Fed policy reasonably well during normal times (Slide 6). I'd note, though, that the Taylor errors in the 1990s are big – actually, bigger than the loudest complaint that John Taylor lodges against the Fed for the 2003–06 violations of the rule.

Of course, the rule completely breaks down during the Great Recession and its aftermath (Slide 7). It says to set the federal funds rate at minus 5 percent in

1.   Ben S. Bernanke, 2011, "Semiannual monetary policy report to the Congress before the Committee on Banking, Housing and Urban Affairs," U.S. Senate, Washington, DC, transcript, March 1, available at http://www.gpo.gov/fdsys/pkg/CHRG-112shrg65824/pdf/CHRG-112shrg65824.pdf.

2009. We can't do that. Moreover, there is no emergency handbook that comes with the rule that says what to do in this event. The effective policy rule is really the maximum of zero and the prescription from real rates and output and inflation gaps. We are thus left with inaction, and inaction looks like policy abdication and a failure to make timely progress in reducing policy imbalances. In these cases, this "policy rule" fails to provide clear policy intentions to achieve goals in a timely fashion and it fails to produce accountability at the zero lower bound. This rule cannot be the be all and end all — for a policy rule that some suggest should govern the implementation of monetary policy in the U.S., this is an absolute failure.

Taylor (1999) Rule During Normal Times

Slide 6

Furthermore, once the rule has failed, and done so for so long, how can we be confident that its prescriptions will still be a good policy to follow once the rule says that the fed funds rate should rise above zero again? More generally, it is difficult to figure out how to jury-rig work-arounds for these simple rules, because they often have a loose and ad hoc relationship between economic theory and the right-hand-side variables and parameters. It is particularly disconcerting that simple Taylor-type rules are typically offered without an explicit theoretical underpinning for the rule. Consider Taylor1993.

This specification follows a "rule of 2s:" 2 percent inflation objective relative to pre-1992 experience, 2 percent equilibrium real interest rate and parameter weights of ½.

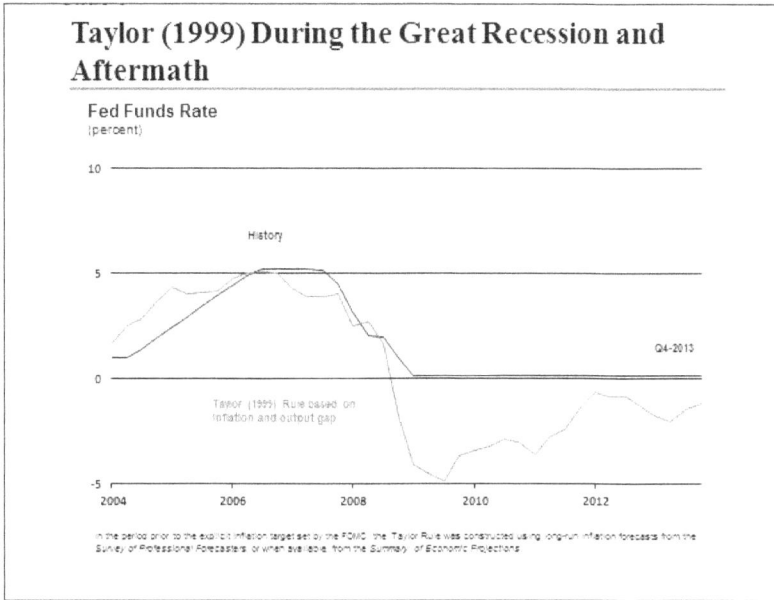

Taylor (1999) During the Great Recession and Aftermath

Slide 7

The resulting constant intercept term in the rule is particularly vexing. It is well known that policy actions that fail to account for the time-varying nature of the natural rate of unemployment can lead to seriously inappropriate monetary outcomes — like double- digit inflation in the 1970s. Just as relevantly, it is well known that the equilibrium real interest rate is not a constant. However, the Taylor rule sets this intercept at 2 percent — a constant. How is this less egregious than simply assuming that the natural rate of unemployment is always 4 percent? Consider Larry Summers' recent hypothesis that the U.S. may be facing a secular stagnation, which would contemplate a lower and perhaps negative equilibrium real rate. Maybe that is a small risk, but it has an extraordinarily high policy loss associated with the wrong robotic prescriptions for policy. According to Mehra and Prescott (1985), the historical average short-term real interest rate is less than 1 percent, with large variations over the long period they study.[2]

As I mentioned earlier, the Bernanke FOMC has worked hard to make the Fed's policy intentions clear and provide accountability for our nontraditional policy actions to support more timely achievement of our goals. With the January 2012 long-run policy strategy, policy intentions are explicit: Get to bull's-eye

---

2.   R. Mehra and E. C. Prescott, 1985, "The equity premium: A puzzle," Journal of Monetary Economics, Vol. 15, March, pp. 145-161. It is worth noting that updating the Mehra and Prescott results to include the more recent period yields similar results – low average real short-term interest rates with large swings across decades.

with labor market near 5½ percent unemployment rate and PCE inflation at 2 percent. When the federal funds rate is stuck at zero and goal-oriented monetary policy says do more — Do more! The quantitative-easing programs and enhanced forward guidance on short-term interest rates reflect a commitment to a clear policy principle. The Bernanke FOMC's attention to policy misses has been vigilant throughout. And so the misses have led us to numerous policy interventions: QE1 in March 2009; QE2 in fall 2010; the forward guidance in August 2011; Operation Twist in fall 2011; the open-ended QE3 in fall 2012; and the threshold forward guidance in December 2012. What is the accountability test? Although much has been done — looking at the bull's-eye scorecard — if anything, the FOMC has been less aggressive than the policy loss function might admit.

Despite the enhancements in recent years, there are remaining communications challenges regarding Fed policy intentions. The Fed has demonstrated that it will act aggressively to reduce resource slack when it is well away from its objective. It is less clear the public understands that we should be willing to overshoot our objectives in order to more speedily re-attain our goals. A slow glide toward our goals from large imbalances risks being stymied along the way and is more likely to fail if adverse shocks hit beforehand. The surest and quickest way to get to the objective is to be willing to overshoot in a manageable fashion. With regard to our inflation objective, we need to repeatedly state clearly that our 2 percent objective is not a ceiling for inflation. Our "balanced approach" to reducing imbalances clearly indicates our symmetric attitudes toward our 2 percent inflation objective.

Let me point out another misperception regarding our inflation objective (Slide 8). It must be noted repeatedly that our 2 percent inflation objective is for the PCE price index. The more popular Consumer Price Index (CPI) tends to run about a quarter to a half point higher on average than the PCE index. Accordingly, this implies that price stability in terms of CPI inflation is higher, closer to 2½ percent. This is particularly important to note since a number of useful measures such as the Treasury Inflation Protected Securities (TIPS) inflation compensation that we and market participants so often refer to is in terms of the higher CPI numbers. Moreover, consumer inflation expectations likely are closer to CPI expectations, since the CPI is restricted to out-of-pocket expenditures and gets used for Social Security adjustments and the like. The PCE price index is the preferred inflation measure on theoretical grounds, and so it is the appropriate index to use for our inflation target; but as policymakers, we should call attention to these inflation measurement discrepancies in order to best communicate our policy intentions and make sure the public correctly interprets our policygoals.

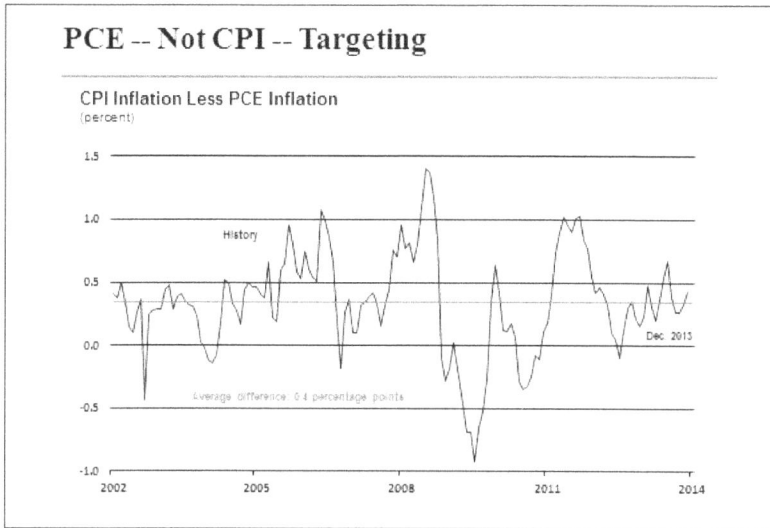

PCE -- Not CPI -- Targeting

CPI Inflation Less PCE Inflation
(percent)

Slide 8

There is a very real risk of confusion on this score. Last Friday, Jon Hilsenrath of the *Wall Street Journal*, who follows Fed communications very closely, mentioned that CPI inflation, at 1.6 percent, was rising a bit and it was getting closer to the Fed's 2 percent objective.[3] That is misleading. Our 2 percent objective is with respect to the PCE index. For the CPI, 2½ percent is a more accurate calibration of our price stability goal.

To conclude, clear communication is key to effective monetary policy strategy. I believe the Fed can meet 90 percent of its communications challenge by seeking to: "Express policy intentions clearly so that the public can understand the Federal Reserve's goals and the Fed's commitment to achieving these goals in a timely fashion."

---

3.   Jon Hilsenrath, 2014, "Grand Central: Maybe inflation isn't as low as Fed thinks," Wall Street Journal, Real Time Economics, blog, February 21, available at http://blogs.wsj.com/economics/2014/02/21/grand-central-maybe- inflation-isnt-as-low-as-fed-thinks/.

U.S. Monetary Policy Forum 2014

Panel discussion on "Lessons for Communications Policy from Our Experiences with Unconventional Monetary Policy"

By Charles I. Plosser

PRESIDENT AND CHIEF EXECUTIVE OFFICER
AT THE FEDERAL RESERVE BANK OF PHILADELPHIA

Highlights

- President Plosser believes the Federal Open Market Committee has to revamp its current forward guidance regarding the future federal funds rate path because the 6.5 percent unemployment threshold has become irrelevant.

- President Plosser points out that before offering new forward guidance, the FOMC ought to be clear about its purpose. Is it purely a transparency device, or is it a way to commit to a more accommodative future policy stance to add more accommodation today?

- President Plosser notes that commitment is required to be successful in either approach to forward guidance. Policymakers cannot maintain discretion and simultaneously commit to forward guidance and expect that guidance to be effective.

Introduction

It is a pleasure to return to this event. The organizers have put together another great and timely program with distinguished participants. However, with Governor Stein and Presidents Kocherlakota, Evans, and myself all here, I am beginning to wonder if we are in Washington rather than in New York. Nevertheless, it is great to be on the program with so many of my fellow policymakers. If you listen carefully to each of us, you will understand why I start with the usual caveat that my remarks represent my own views and not necessarily those of the Federal Reserve System or my colleagues on the Federal Open Market Committee (FOMC).

Communication and transparency have been important themes in monetary policy discussions over the past decade or more. Indeed, in 2007 this Monetary Policy Forum began with Alan Blinder's keynote address titled "Making Monetary Policy and Talking about It." In part, this emphasis on communication and transparency reflects the steady evolution in the theory and science of monetary policy. Reflecting this emerging consensus, the Federal Reserve during the tenure of Chairman Bernanke has taken a number of actions to promote increased transparency about its actions and policies. In fact, President Evans and I served on a subcommittee led by current Chair Yellen specifically focused on improving communication.

Our efforts to improve communication took on heightened importance as the FOMC responded to the financial crisis and recession. Since December 2008, the federal funds rate target has been near zero. Since the nominal funds rate cannot go below zero, we had to develop alternative policy tools in an effort to provide further accommodation to support the recovery. We also had to figure out how and what to communicate about these new tools. Thus, well-understood communication practices about traditional policy tools gave way to untested ways to describe these new tools. The task was further complicated because one of the unconventional tools was so-called forward guidance. Forward guidance seeks to inform the public about the future path of policy rather than describing a policy action taken today. Thus, effective forward guidance is all about communication and what it conveys or doesn't convey.

In my brief time today, I will focus on why I think communication is such a challenge and discuss some of the choices the Committee faces going forward.

Current State of Affairs

First, communication is difficult because monetary policy is more complicated than it used to be. With the traditional policy tool at the zero lower bound, the Committee has focused on two unconventional tools. The first is the purchase of long-term assets, and the second, as I mentioned, is forward guidance. The asset purchase program has had many dimensions, such as the overall volume of purchases, the pace of purchases, the kinds of assets targeted for purchase, and the criteria for starting and stopping the purchases. Policymakers have tried to fine-tune the program along each dimension while assessing the trade-offs among them and the trade-offs with other policy tools, such as the traditional funds rate decision. With so many moving parts to our policy framework, it is not surprising that communication is very complicated.

We are now in the third round of asset purchases, or quantitative easing. Since September 2012, the FOMC has added some $1.3 trillion in long-term Treasuries and mortgage-backed securities to its balance sheet through this program, buying at a pace of $85 billion a month in 2013. This program, known as QE3, is already twice the size of the last round of asset purchases that was initiated in November 2010, known as QE2.

In December 2013, the Committee announced that it would reduce the pace of purchases from $85 billion to $75 billion per month. In January, it announced a further reduction to $65 billion. The FOMC is now on a path of measured reductions, which, if continued, will end the purchase program late this year. If the economy continues to improve, we could find ourselves still trying to increase accommodation in an environment when history suggests that policy should perhaps be moving in the opposite direction.

Communication about the future path of asset purchases has, at times, been imprecise and confusing. Last June, the Committee suggested that it might begin to reduce the pace of purchases in the fall and perhaps end them when the unemployment rate reached 7 percent. However, the Committee did not even begin the tapering process until unemployment had reached 7 percent. It now seems unlikely that the program will end until the unemployment rate is below – or as indicated in the FOMC statement, perhaps "well below" – 6.5 percent.

Why is the 6.5 percent unemployment rate important? Because the Committee made it important. The Committee, in essence, told the markets that the 6.5 percent unemployment rate was an important quantitative marker. In December 2012, the FOMC indicated that it intended to keep the federal funds rate target near zero at least as long as the unemployment rate was above 6.5 percent, the inflation rate between one and two years ahead was projected to be no more than 2.5 percent, and inflation expectations remained well anchored. However, it is important to remember that these guideposts were thresholds, not triggers. The FOMC had not made a commitment to act once a threshold was reached, nor did it indicate how policy would evolve after a threshold was reached. It simply signaled that it would not act prior to crossing one of the thresholds.

Yet, the 6.5 percent threshold will soon become irrelevant, and it probably is already. So the Committee, at a minimum, has to revamp its communications regarding the future federal funds rate path. Given that we are still easing policy by buying assets, it is pretty clear that even though the threshold will soon come and go, the Committee is unlikely to contemplate raising rates as long as it is buying assets. Put another way, the practical constraint at this point for raising the policy rate is no longer the unemployment rate but the fact that we are still buying assets. Indeed, the Committee has acknowledged that it will likely be appropriate to keep rates at their current low rates well past the time unemployment falls below 6.5 percent. Therefore, in my view, the threshold has already lost its meaning as a guidepost. It needs to be replaced with something that is more relevant and informative.

This poses the challenge of how and what to communicate about policy going forward. Our actions and the data have made the current form of forward guidance outdated and mostly irrelevant. Indeed, one could reasonably wonder whether the inflation threshold has any meaning at this point. In other words, by allowing the unemployment threshold to pass without taking action, the public might conclude that the Committee could easily decide to let the inflation threshold pass without taking action as well.

Competing Roles for Forward Guidance

Before we offer further forward guidance, it is important to be clear about what this forward guidance is intended to accomplish. As Yogi Berra is reported to have said, "You have to be careful if you don't know where you're going because you might

end up somewhere else."

One way to think of forward guidance is that it is just another step toward increased transparency and effective communication of monetary policy. This approach seeks to clarify how policymakers will alter policy as economic conditions change, that is, to describe a reaction function. By being more transparent about how policy will evolve as a function of economic conditions, this approach can help the public form more accurate expectations about the future path of monetary policy.

Economists have learned that expectations play an important role in determining economic outcomes. When businesses and households have a better understanding of how monetary policy is likely to evolve, they can make more informed spending and financial decisions. If monetary policymakers can reduce uncertainty about the course of monetary policy, the economy is likely to perform more efficiently.

Of course, in order to communicate something about the reaction function, you have to have one. That means in order to be successful with this approach to forward guidance, policymakers must be able to agree on how they will systematically respond to changes in economic conditions. To be useful, however, the reaction function need not be mechanistic. Qualitative information about such a function and how it will be implemented can also be useful and meaningful. Nevertheless, some degree of commitment to abide by the specified reaction function is necessary, if the communication is to achieve the desired result of reducing policy uncertainty and providing meaningful forward guidance. The excuse that "this time is different" undermines the commitment and the credibility of the information that the communication is seeking to provide. I would add that a committed and credible approach to such a systematic approach to policy is helpful and informative regardless of whether you are at the zero lower bound or not.

A somewhat different rationale or view of forward guidance is that it is a way of increasing accommodation in a period when the policy rate is at or near the zero lower bound. Some models suggest that when you are at the zero lower bound, it can be desirable, or optimal, to indicate that future policy rates will be kept "lower for longer" than might otherwise be the case. Thus, policymakers intentionally commit to deviating from what they would otherwise choose to do in normal times, such as following the Taylor rule. In these models, such a commitment would tend to raise inflation expectations and lower long-term nominal rates, thereby inducing households and businesses to spend more today.

This approach asks more of forward guidance than just articulating a reaction function. It takes more credibility and commitment because it requires policymakers to directly influence and manage the public's beliefs about the future policy path in ways that are different from how they may have behaved in the past. As I have indicated in previous speeches, this approach to forward guidance can backfire if the policy is misunderstood.[1] For example, if the public hears that the policy rate will be lower for longer, it may interpret this news as policymakers saying that they expect the economy to be weaker for longer. If that is the interpretation of the message, then the forward guidance will not succeed and may even weaken current spending.

The FOMC has not been clear about the purpose of its forward guidance. Is it purely a transparency device, or is it a way to commit to a more accommodative future policy stance to add more accommodation today? This lack of clarity makes it difficult to communicate the stance of policy and the conditionality of policy on the state of the economy.

Note that most formulations of standard, simple policy rules suggest that the federal funds rate should rise very soon – if not already. In other words, the zero lower bound no longer appears to be binding. However, the FOMC has provided forward guidance indicating that the federal funds rate will need to be low for some time to come.

How do we reconcile this apparent incongruity? It could be that the FOMC is using its forward guidance as a commitment device or signal for a more accommodative policy well into the future, as in the second approach I have discussed. Or, it could be the FOMC views forward guidance as a device for increased transparency but that it doesn't think the standard rules apply in the current environment. Then what rules do apply? If policymakers are not relying on a rule or a rule-like reaction function, policy is purely discretionary and forward guidance becomes ineffective. In either case, we have an opportunity and an obligation to provide more transparency and better communication.

This leads me to suggest that there is a more fundamental tension underlying our forward guidance and communication challenges. Forward guidance in either of the two approaches that I have discussed requires a degree of commitment to conduct future policy in some particular manner. That commitment is central to the success of either approach. Yet, I would suggest that the old "rules versus discretion"

---

1.   See Charles I. Plosser, "Forward Guidance," speech to the Stanford Institute for Economic Policy Research's (SIEPR) Associates Meeting, February 12, 2013, Stanford, CA

debate is alive and well. This, of course, is not a new tension within the FOMC, nor is it one that is likely to go away in the near term. But the heightened weight and prominence given to forward guidance as a policy tool has certainly shined a spotlight on this longstanding debate.

The desire to maintain flexibility to respond to "events on the ground" is a strong one. One can make the case that discretion is deeply ingrained in most policy institutions, particularly the Fed. Yet, the desire to maintain discretion is anathema to the commitment required for successful forward guidance. Policymakers cannot maintain discretion and simultaneously commit to forward guidance and expect that guidance to be effective.

So, I conclude as I began: Forward guidance and clear communications remain important challenges for monetary policymakers.

U.S. Monetary Policy Forum 2014

Panel discussion on "Lessons for Communications Policy from Our Experiences with Unconventional Monetary Policy"

Communication and Forward Guidance
in a World of Unconventional Monetary Policy:
The Case of the Bank of Japan

By Sayuri Shirai

MEMBER OF THE POLICY BOARD, BANK OF JAPAN

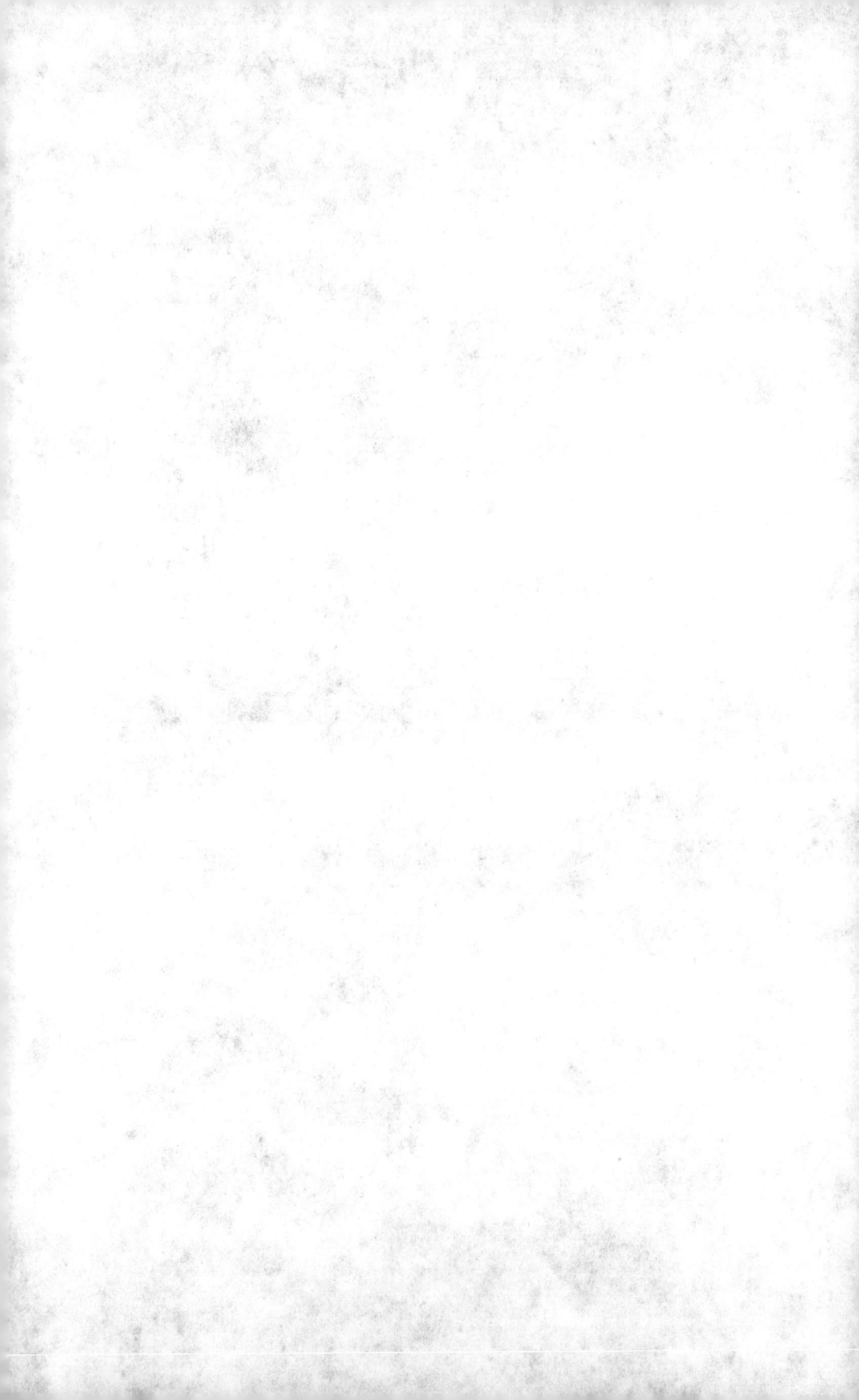

I. Introduction

Thank you very much for inviting me to the 2014 U.S. Monetary Policy Forum. I feel greatly honored to have the opportunity to talk about communication on monetary policy in the context of the Bank of Japan.

As you may know, the Bank adopted *quantitative and qualitative monetary easing* (QQE) in April 2013. Prior to this, the Bank had adopted the 2 percent price stability target in terms of the year-on-year rate of change in the consumer price index (CPI) in January 2013. The Bank committed to pursuing monetary easing to achieve the 2 percent target as early as possible. Despite this increased transparency on its inflation target, some in both the markets and the public soon questioned the achievability of the 2 percent target under the then existing monetary easing framework called *comprehensive monetary easing* (CME) adopted in October 2010. This appears to have reflected (1) a perception of lack of boldness under CME,[1] (2) doubt about the Bank's determination to overcome deflation due to ineffective communication between the Bank and the markets as well as the public, and (3) disbelief arising from the Bank's past monetary policy because of a poor track record in achieving its stated objectives.[2] Under these conditions, QQE was introduced in April 2013.

Given this background, my presentation will begin by touching on the main features of QQE. I will then explain the Bank's forward guidance, or its communication strategy, on its future monetary policy stance. Finally, I will discuss issues related to the Bank's communication on monetary policy.

II. Main Features of QQE and the Bank's Forward Guidance

Let me first highlight some distinctive differences between the current QQE and the previous CME (Chart 1).

---

1. The size of the Asset Purchase Program was increased nine times, each time in the range of 5-10 trillion yen. The purchase of JGBs was mainly up to a remaining maturity of three years.

2. This often refers to the exit timings of the *zero interest rate policy* in August 2000 and *quantitative monetary easing* in March 2006.

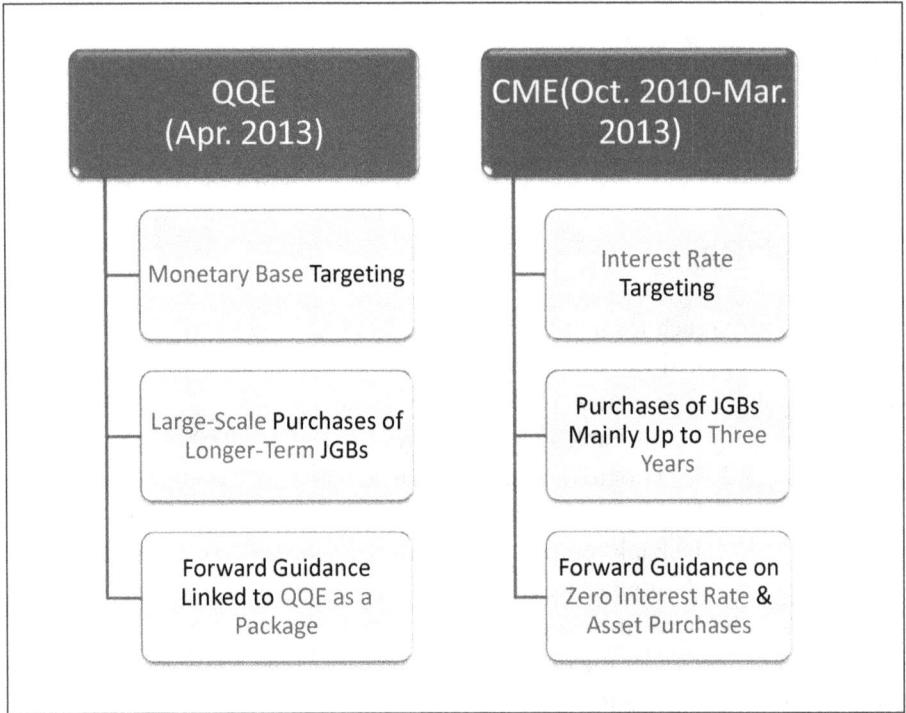

Chart 1

Shifting from Interest Rate Targeting to Monetary Base Targeting

First, the main feature of QQE was a shift in the main operating target for money market operations from the *uncollateralized overnight call rate* to the *monetary base*. There were several reasons for this shift. It was thought it would be intuitively easier for the public to grasp the essence of monetary easing: an increase in the "quantity" could easily be connected to a large-scale supply of cash, creating an image of inflation. Moreover, market participants use the monetary base as a reference for measuring the scale of monetary easing across central banks when engaging in financial transactions. Certain academic research studies were also taken into account in regard to the Bank's adoption of monetary base targeting.[3] Moreover, there was general agreement among the Policy Board members that changing the main operating target would effectively signal a much-needed change in the monetary policy framework and enable the Bank to wipe away its image as a reluctant monetary accommodator. Hence, the shift was decided as part of the Bank's *communication policy tool*. The purchase of Japanese

---

3.   These research studies, including those related to the Bank's monetary policy, include Paul R. Krugman, "It's Baaack: Japan's Slump and the Return of the Liquidity Trap," *Brookings Papers on Economic Activity*, 1998, 2, pp. 137-205; Allan H. Meltzer, "The Transmission Process," paper presented to the Deutsche Bundesbank

government bonds (JGBs) was viewed as the main tool to fulfill the monetary base target. The Bank now purchases JGBs with a remaining maturity from a minimum of less than one year up to the maximum 40 years.

Importance of Raising Long-Term Inflation Expectations

Here, I should also mention that QQE relies more heavily on long-term inflation expectations to achieve negative long-term real interest rates than the monetary policies adopted by other central banks. A decline in long-term interest rates in real terms may increase investment and consumption. The anticipation of higher inflation may hasten such increases. These expectations may also affect current sales prices and wages. Thus, the Bank decided to use all available tools to convince the markets and the public of its strong determination to overcome mild deflation and to help transform the deflation-oriented mindset. In this spirit, the "quantity"-based targeting approach was considered reasonable. This feature draws a clear line between QQE and the previous CME, which placed little emphasis on influencing such expectations and perceptions relating to the Bank's monetary policy stance.

The Bank's Communication Strategy
and Two Descriptions in Its Forward Guidance

QQE entails forward guidance as one of its most important elements (Chart 2). The Bank released a *public statement* in April 2013 that introduced QQE, and contained two descriptions of the time span of monetary accommodation. The first description was a statement of the Bank's intention to achieve the 2 percent price stability target *at the earliest possible time, with a time horizon of about two years*. The second description was a statement of its intention to continue with QQE as long as it was necessary for *maintaining the 2 percent target in a stable manner*. This description also added a condition that both upside and downside risks to economic activity and prices would be examined, and that adjustments would be made as appropriate.

The purpose of the first description was to signal to both the markets and the public the Bank's intention to achieve its 2 percent target within a time horizon of about two years, normally pursued by other central banks under an inflation targeting framework. The reason the Bank set a time span was to show its determination

Conference on the Monetary Transmission Process: Recent Developments and Lessons for Europe, 1999; Ben S. Bernanke, "Japanese Monetary Policy: A Case of Self-Induced Paralysis?" in Adam Posen and Ryoichi Mikitani, eds. *Japan's Financial Crisis and Its Parallels to U.S. Experience*, Special Report 13, Institute for International Economics, Washington, D.C., 2000, pp. 149-166; and Bennett T. McCallum, "Alternative Monetary Policy Rules: A Comparison with Historical Settings for the United States, the United Kingdom, and Japan," *Economic Quarterly*, Federal Reserve Bank of Richmond, 2000, pp. 49-79.

to achieve the target and increase the confidence of the markets and the public. To fulfill this objective, the main operating target for money market operations was switched from the uncollateralized overnight call rate to the monetary base; it was then decided that the size of the monetary base would rise at an annual pace of about 60-70 trillion yen, to be doubled in two calendar years (2013-14). Under this monetary base target, the Bank currently purchases JGBs of approximately 50 trillion yen (on an outstanding basis) each year to double the amount outstanding in two years (Chart 3).

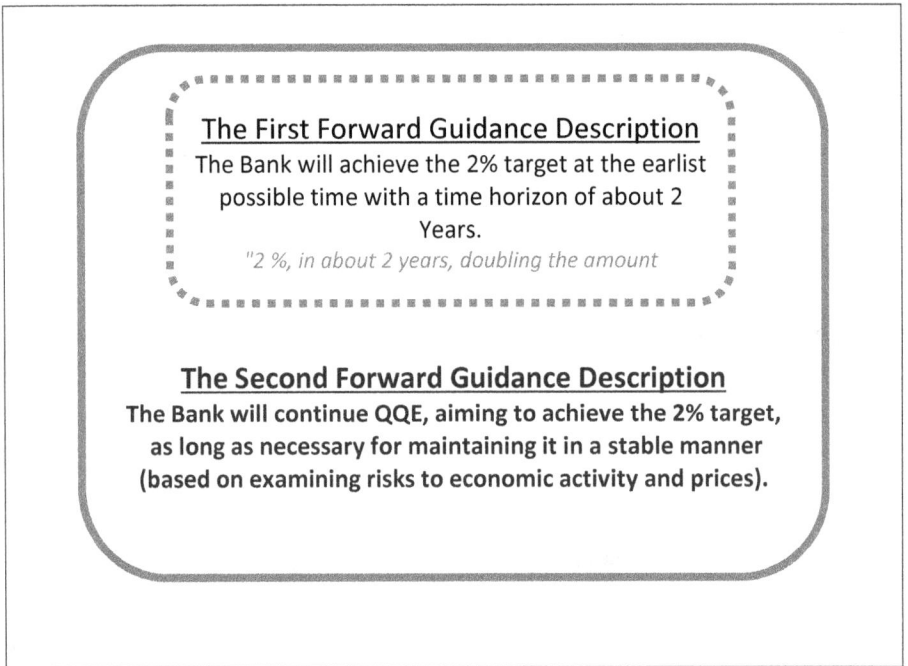

The First Forward Guidance Description
The Bank will achieve the 2% target at the earlist possible time with a time horizon of about 2 Years.
"2 %, in about 2 years, doubling the amount

The Second Forward Guidance Description
The Bank will continue QQE, aiming to achieve the 2% target, as long as necessary for maintaining it in a stable manner (based on examining risks to economic activity and prices).

Chart 2

Some market participants considered that the first description is a strong *calendar-based commitment*. This may have partly reflected an impression gained from the Bank's communication about QQE in April 2013. Namely, the Bank stressed the number "two" on many occasions -- *the 2 percent price stability target, a time horizon of about two years, doubling the monetary base and the amount outstanding of JGBs, and more than doubling the average remaining maturity of JGB purchases.* This presentation was successful in sending a clear message about the new framework. However, the message may also have been interpreted by some market participants as a strong *calendar-based* commitment with a time limit, with a lesser focus on the second description (which I will describe in a moment). Personally, I believe that the first description could be interpreted as both *calendar-based* (about two years) as well as *state-contingent* (2 percent) guidances. However, in this case, the time horizon of "about two years" should be interpreted with some flexibility rather than as a rigid "two years."

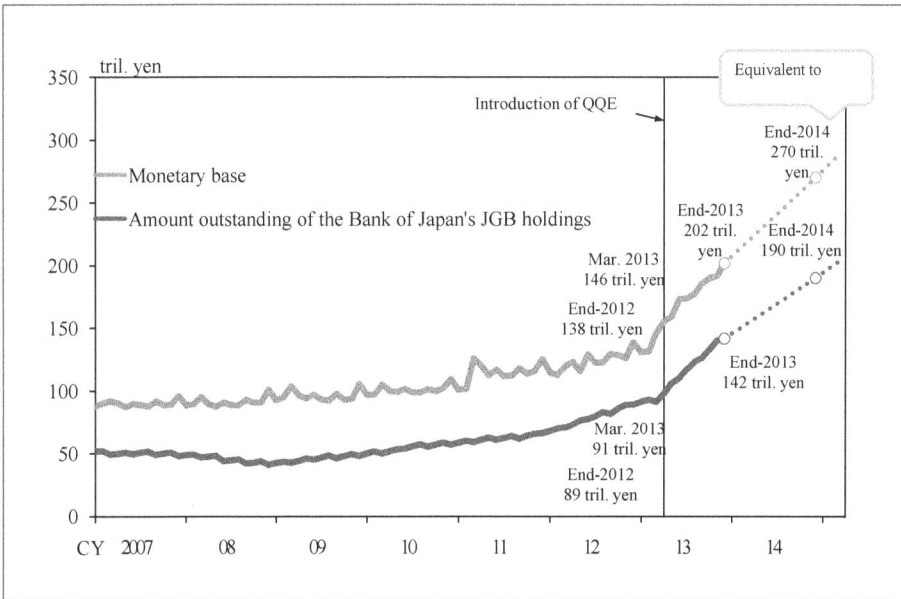

Chart 3

The <u>second description</u> is related to a *conditional commitment*, because the continuation of QQE is subject to the examination of upside and downside risk factors. It is also *state-contingent* guidance (to maintain the 2 percent target in a stable manner), linked to the continuation of QQE, and it plays a greater role than the first description in stabilizing long-term inflation expectations at around 2 percent. This helps to reduce long-term interest rate volatility and prevent its overshooting.

The first description can be considered as a "necessary condition" for achieving the second description, if the first description is regarded as referring to the achievability of the 2 percent target and the second as referring to the maintenance of the 2 percent target in a stable manner. While the time horizon of these two descriptions could overlap, the second description implies that the time horizon is somewhat longer and that the asset purchases may not come to an end after two years. In this sense, the QQE time framework may be described as "open-ended," although the April 2013 *public statement* stipulated the annual pace of increase in the monetary base for the coming two calendar years. Thus, these two descriptions are mutually non-exclusive.

Based on the framework I have described, the Bank holds the baseline scenario that core CPI inflation (CPI for all items less fresh food; excluding the direct effects of the consumption tax hikes) is expected to reach around 2 percent toward the latter half of the projection period of fiscal 2013-15.[4]

Personally, I am aware of the possibility that it may take some time to achieve the 2 percent target, since the duration depends crucially on *"the pace of improvement in the employment and income situation in Japan."* Moreover, it is possible that it may take even longer to achieve a situation where the 2 percent target is maintained in a stable manner, considering the duration required to judge whether the condition described as "in a stable manner" is met. During this period, support from monetary policy is likely to be necessary. Bear in mind here that the Bank adopted the 2 percent target in January 2013, assuming that such an inflation rate should be *sustainable.*[5] Hence, the Bank's decisions on the necessity and measures of future monetary easing should be judged in line with the objective to pursue a society with 2 percent price increase in a stable manner.

Why Is the Bank's Forward Guidance So Different from That of the Federal Reserve?

The form of forward guidance adopted by the Bank differs from that of the Federal Reserve on several fronts (Chart 4). First, the Federal Reserve applies forward guidance to its primary short-term policy interest rate (the overnight federal funds rate) and provides guidance to the markets and the public about how long it expects to keep the current exceptionally low level. In other words, the Federal Reserve attempts to exert downward pressure on longer-term interest rates by influencing expectations of the markets and the public regarding the continuation of the current low level of short-term interest rates over an extended period of time. Asset purchases are regarded as a *separate* monetary easing policy tool and are supplementing the interest rate policy and forward guidance. In contrast, the Bank applies forward guidance to QQE as a package. Once the pace of the annual increase in the monetary base is set, the approximate pace of increase in JGB purchases is determined accordingly. In this sense, the pace of increase in the monetary base and that in asset purchases are treated as

---

4.   The consumption tax rate in Japan is scheduled to increase from 5 percent to 8 percent in April 2014 and further to 10 percent in October 2015. The hikes are expected to raise CPI-based inflation by about 2 percentage points for fiscal 2014 and by 0.7 percentage point for fiscal 2015, respectively. When assessing the inflation rate, the Bank disregards the effects of these increases as they are temporary.

5.   The *Joint Statement of the Government and the Bank of Japan on Overcoming Deflation and Achieving Sustainable Economic Growth*, released in January 2013, stated, "The Bank recognizes that the inflation rate consistent with price stability on a sustainable basis will rise as efforts by a wide range of entities toward strengthening competitiveness and growth potential of Japan's economy make progress." Based on this recognition, the Bank set the 2 percent target.

"*non-separable*," as shown in Chart 3. Then the Bank uses forward guidance to inform the public of its intention to maintain an increase in the monetary base and thus in asset purchases in the future. In other words, the Bank attempts to exert downward pressure on the entire yield curve by influencing the expectations of the markets and the public about the low level of the yield curve in the future.

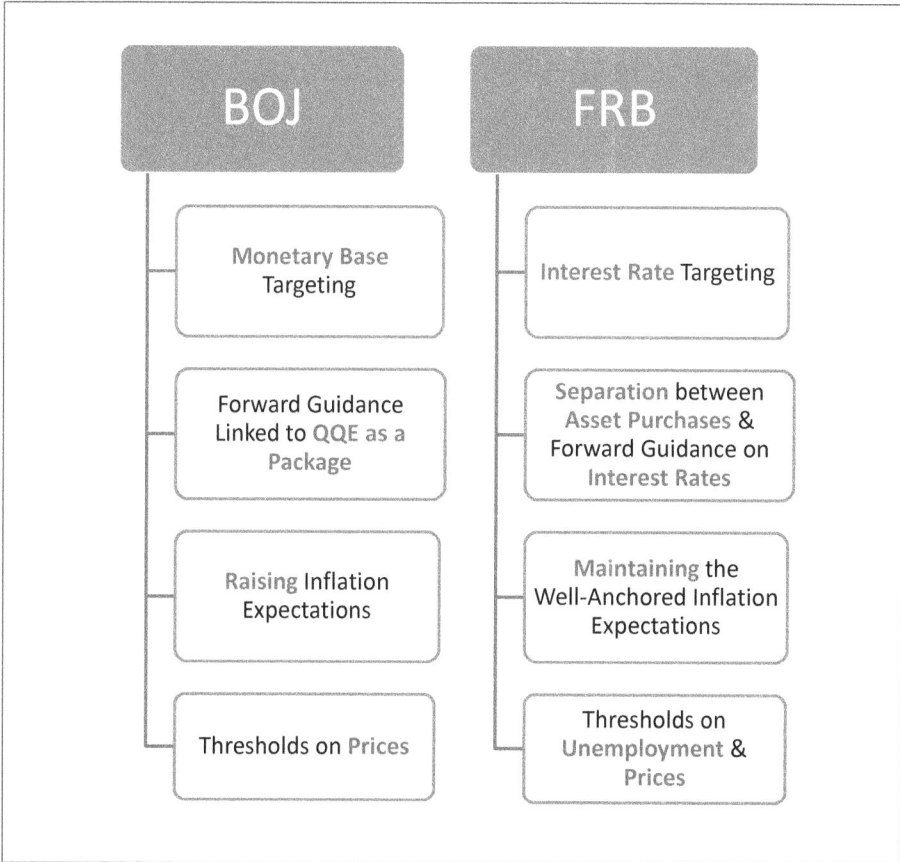

BOJ	FRB
Monetary Base Targeting	Interest Rate Targeting
Forward Guidance Linked to QQE as a Package	Separation between Asset Purchases & Forward Guidance on Interest Rates
Raising Inflation Expectations	Maintaining the Well-Anchored Inflation Expectations
Thresholds on Prices	Thresholds on Unemployment & Prices

Chart 4

Second, the Bank purchases treasury discount bills (T-Bills) and other assets, in addition to JGBs, to meet the monetary base target.[6] Moreover, it regularly conducts fixed-rate funds-supplying operations (with a duration of mainly three months, but available up to one year). Therefore, these short-term operations exert

---

6.   Other assets include exchange-traded funds (ETFs), Japan real estate investment trusts (J-REITs), CP, and corporate bonds. The Bank has also charged 0.1 percent on excess reserves since October 2008. Thus, this interest rate functions largely as a floor for the interbank market interest rates.

downward pressure directly on short-term interest rates. In contrast, the Federal Reserve purchases longer-term Treasury securities (with a remaining maturity from four to 30 years) and agency mortgage-backed securities (MBSs). The downward pressure on short-term interest rates is exerted through the forward guidance.

Third, the Bank and the Federal Reserve have different views on long-term inflation expectations. Forward guidance issued by the Federal Reserve assumes that longer-term inflation expectations have been *anchored* at around 2 percent. However, there may be some limited concerns on the dis-anchoring of inflation expectations. Therefore, one of the main tasks for the Federal Reserve is to continue with monetary easing measures to seek economic improvement, while ensuring that the anchored inflation expectations are maintained. In contrast, the Bank has *not yet* successfully anchored long-term inflation expectations at around 2 percent. Thus, the Bank must help transform the deflation-oriented mindset of all economic entities and then increase inflation expectations to a higher level of 2 percent. Therefore, the threshold used for forward guidance concentrates solely on "2 percent" or "maintaining 2 percent in a stable manner."

Fourth, Federal Reserve forward guidance includes employment-related thresholds. It has a dual mandate of promoting price stability and maximum employment, so the reason for this is clear. In contrast, the Bank's primary mandate is to achieve price stability and there is relatively small concern about the unemployment rate. In fact, the unemployment rate for December 2013 reached 3.7 percent, close to the lowest point in recent years of 3.6 percent, which was attained in July 2007. Some labor issues exist, such as the differential treatment of regular and non-regular workers and firms' demand for increased flexibility over labor market regulations. However, these are structural issues that are beyond the scope of monetary policy.

III. Communication and Challenges Faced by the Bank

As you may know, Japan's economy is performing relatively well and the *core* CPI turned positive in June 2013 and reached 1.3 percent in December 2013. Together with expansionary fiscal measures and a front-loaded increase in consumption, QQE has contributed to the favorable performance. That said, I will present my own views on some possible communication-related challenges that the Bank may face in the future.

Maintaining Low Levels of Real Interest Rates and Communicating with the Markets

One clear achievement of QQE (and of the anticipated greater monetary easing from the end of 2012) is that long-term real interest rates turned negative and have

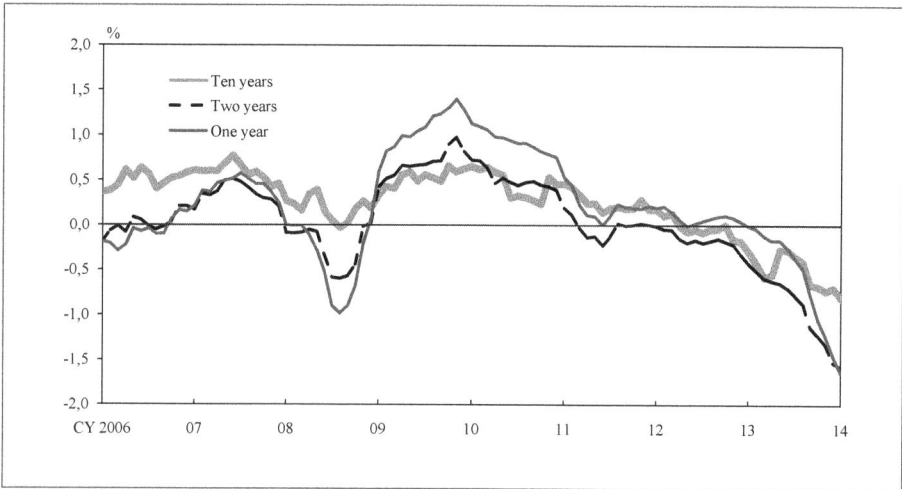

Chart 5

remained in negative territory (Chart 5). This reflects two factors. One factor is the continuous downward pressure being exerted on long-term nominal interest rates. Chart 6 shows that upward pressure on long-term interest rates remains limited to date, since the massive purchases of JGBs have helped to generate strong down-

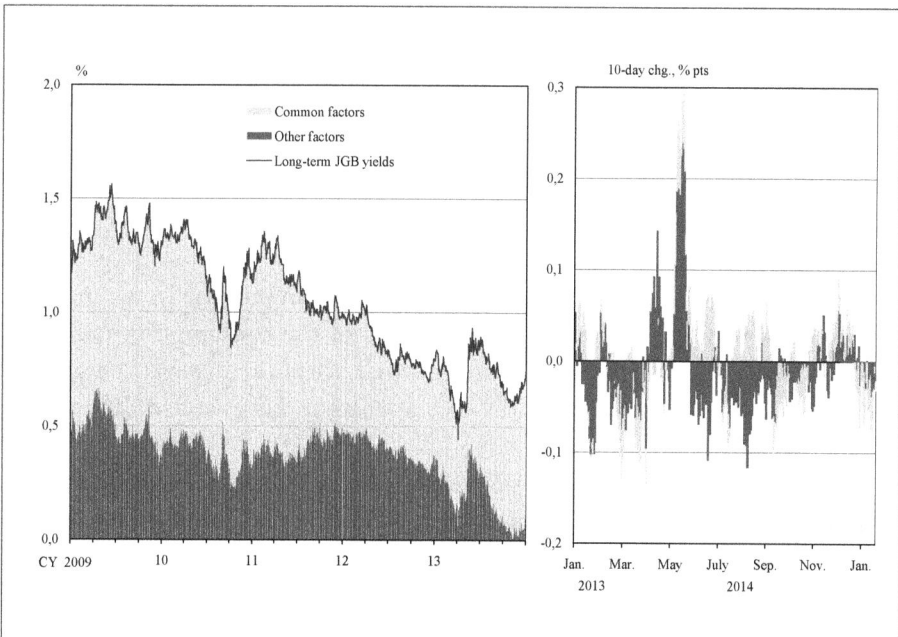

Chart 6

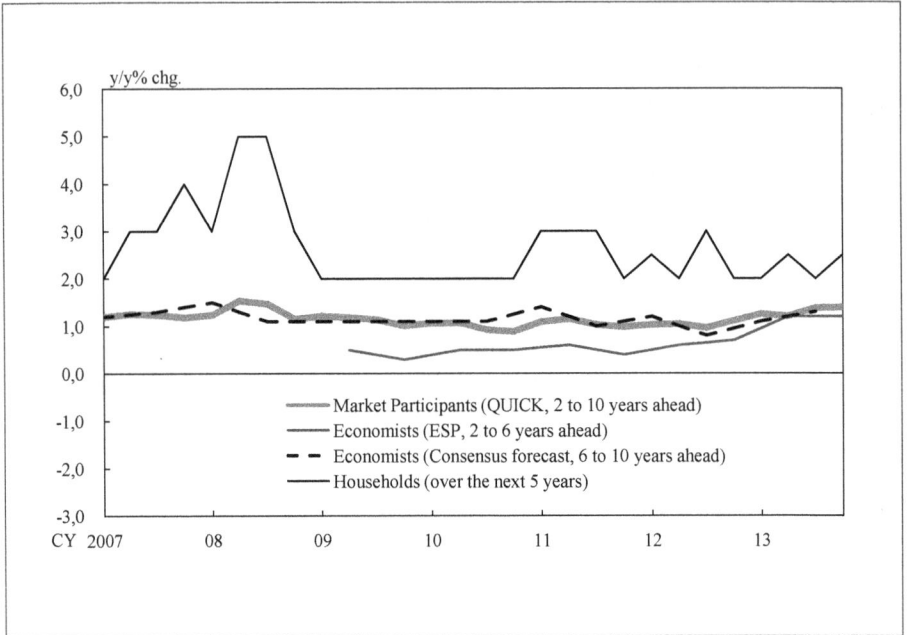

Chart 7

ward pressure on interest rates. The chart shows the decomposition of key factors contributing to long-term JGB yields. It indicates that in recent months downward forces caused by "other factors" (which seems to largely reflect domestic factors) have been greater than upward pressure caused by "common factors" (which largely reflects global factors).

Another factor is an increase in long-term inflation expectations since late 2012. Chart 7 shows survey-based indicators (such expectations of households, economists, and market participants), while Chart 8 shows market data-based indicators. These indicators show a general increase in inflation expectations. However, they require caution in interpretation, as an increase in the inflation expectations may reflect the potential impacts of the consumption tax hikes. After *excluding* the tax effects, they are still well below the 2 percent target and the recent movement of some indicators appears to have leveled off to some extent.

A current and future challenge relates to the growing linkages across financial markets. A rise in long-term nominal government bond yields in a major overseas economy may exert upward pressure on the government bond yields in Japan. The upward force may work against the downward pressure maintained by QQE, potentially weakening the effectiveness of monetary policy and leading to greater volatility in long-term nominal and real interest rates. Yet, even in the phase of intensified upward

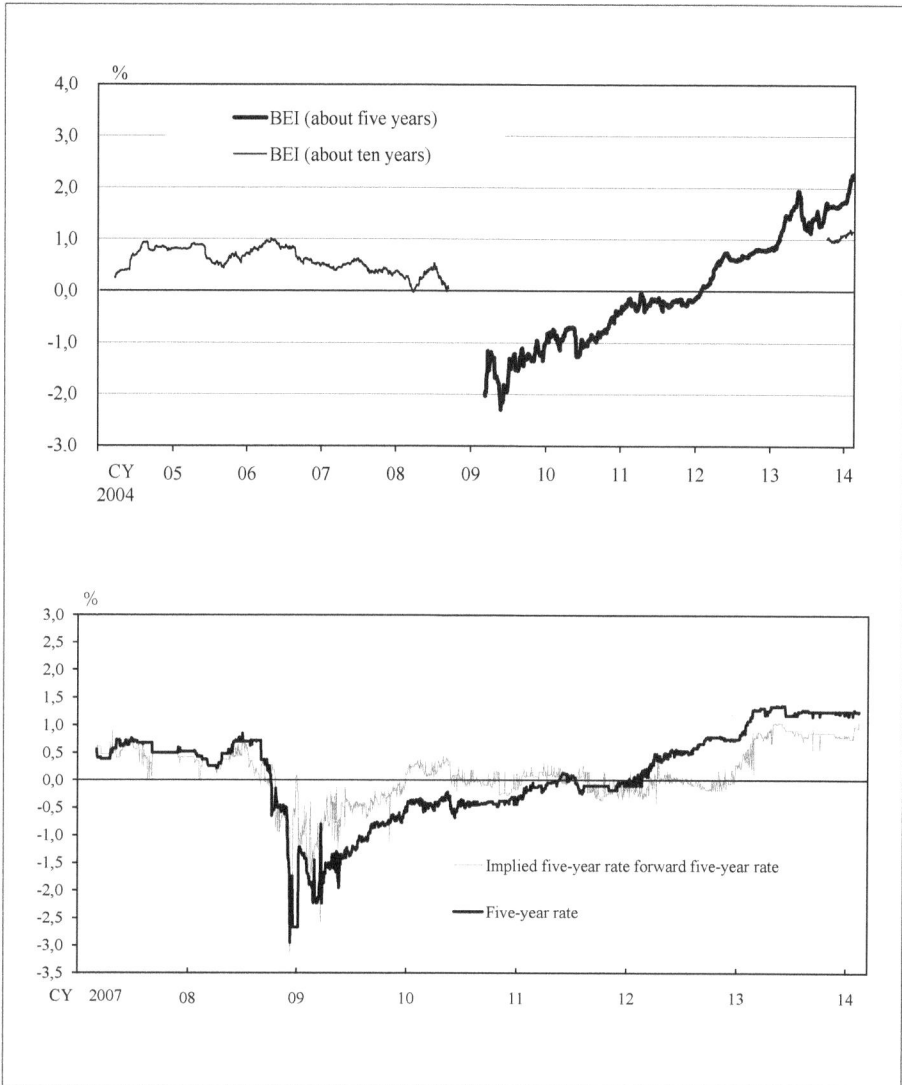

Chart 8

pressure, the continuation of the Bank's large-scale asset purchases is likely to maintain the downward pressure -- in addition to the forward guidance applied to QQE. As long as the rising pace of long-term interest rates is more *moderate* than that of inflation expectations, real interest rates are likely to remain at low levels. Maintaining relatively low levels of nominal and real interest rates as well as contained volatilities are important in terms of supporting the economic recovery path. While the Bank expects that both short- and long-term interest rates will move largely on a stable path, it is important to continue dialogues with the market participants regarding the framework of QQE. Indeed, during April-July 2013, when the JGB market became unstable, the Bank held several dialogues with market participants and adopted a flexible operational framework, which helped to stabilize the market.

Inflation Outlook Gap between the Bank and Economists, and Promotion of Communication with the Latter

As mentioned earlier, according to the Bank's baseline scenario, the core CPI infla-tion (*excluding* the direct effects of the consumption tax hikes) is projected to reach around 2 percent toward the latter half of the projection period of fiscal 2013-15. As shown in Chart 9, the median of the Policy Board members' forecasts is 0.7 percent for fiscal 2013, 1.3 percent for fiscal 2014 (3.3 percent *including* the effects of the tax hike), and 1.9 percent for fiscal 2015 (2.6 percent *including* the effects of the tax hike).[7]

Now let me show you the projections on core CPI-based inflation envisaged by about 40 economists. Chart 10 shows the evolution of the economists' forecasts for inflation (*including* the tax effects) over the period of fiscal 2013-15 by plotting the distribution of their forecasts for each fiscal year. It reveals that the economists' forecasts for inflation were adjusted toward the higher levels with greater probabil-ity for fiscal 2013 as the observation point approached the end of the observation year concerned. A similar but more moderate pattern was present for fiscal 2014. The chart indicates that a divergence of views was also present among economists for fiscal 2014 and 2015. Next, a comparison was made between the average of the economists' forecasts and the median of the Bank's Policy Board members' fore-casts. Chart 11 indicates that a clear convergence was present for fiscal 2013, as a result of adjustments made mainly by the economists. A moderate degree of con-vergence was also observed for fiscal 2014, while a relatively large difference still remained between the projections for fiscal 2015.

The observations I have described suggest that a degree of uncertainty exists re-garding the path toward 2 percent and the time it will take to achieve the 2 percent target. These differences appear to reflect differing views between the Bank and economists, with respect to (1) the pace of improvement in the employment and income situation in Japan, (2) the pace of the rise in long-term inflation expecta-tions, and (3) the ability of firms to raise their sales prices owing to the healthier prospects for profitability.

The views of economists and market participants are particularly important for the Bank. This is because financial markets influence the behavior of households

---

7.   There is a large gap between the maximum and minimum Policy Board member inflation forecasts, suggest-
      ing the presence of divergent views. This divergence widens somewhat for fiscal 2015.

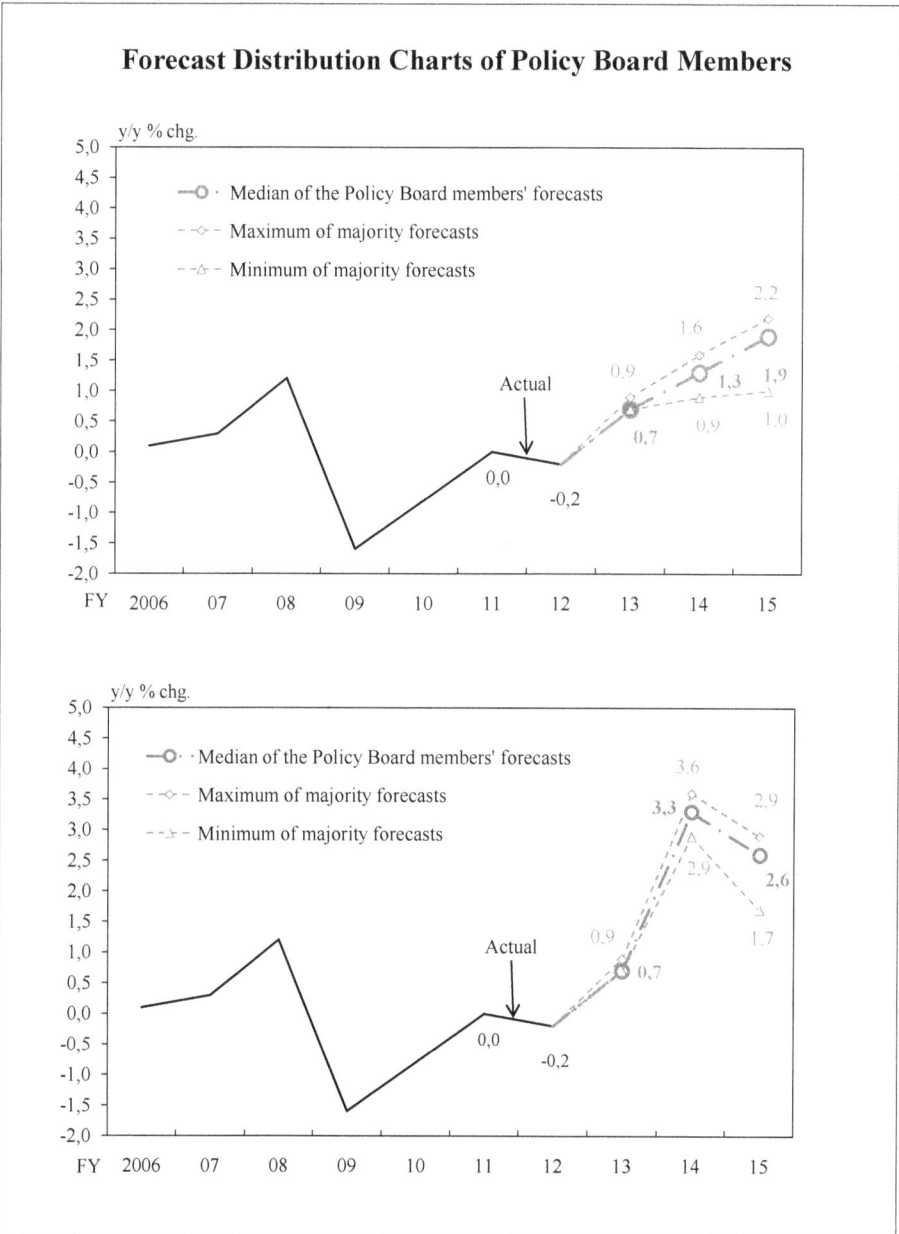

Forecast Distribution Charts of Policy Board Members

y/y % chg.

- Median of the Policy Board members' forecasts
- Maximum of majority forecasts
- Minimum of majority forecasts

Actual

2.2
1.6
0.9   1.3   1.9
0.0
-0.2   0.7   0.9   1.0

FY 2006 07 08 09 10 11 12 13 14 15

y/y % chg.

- Median of the Policy Board members' forecasts
- Maximum of majority forecasts
- Minimum of majority forecasts

Actual

3.6
3.3   2.9
2.9   2.6
0.9
0.0   0.7   1.7
-0.2

FY 2006 07 08 09 10 11 12 13 14 15

Chart 9

and firms through changes in interest rates, foreign exchange rates, and financial as-set prices, but these financial market indicators reflect the valuations of economists and market participants for various financial assets as well as their expectations of future inflation and economic developments. These financial indicators respond

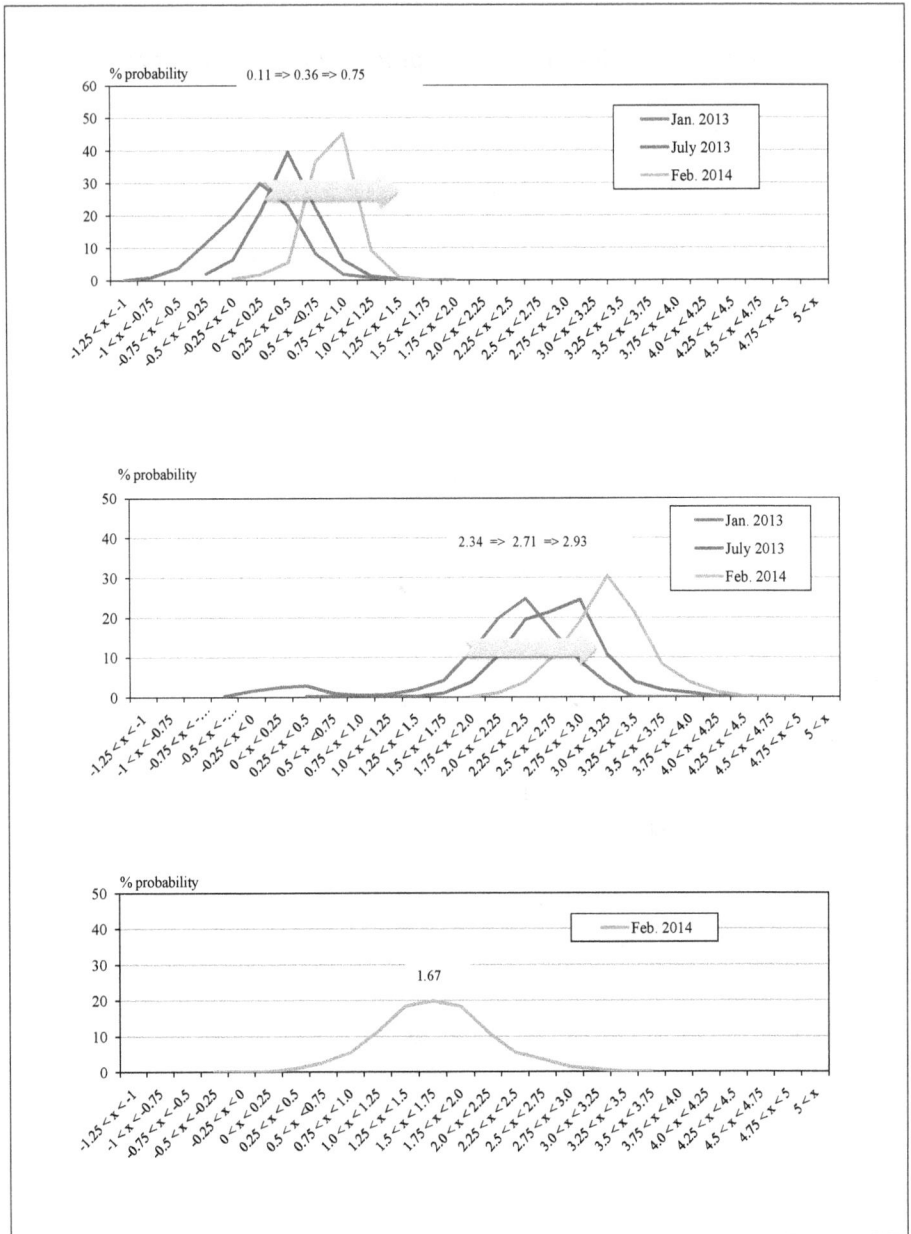

Chart 10

directly to changes in market conditions caused by (present and anticipated) monetary policy measures, in addition to the release of the latest macroeconomic data, news, and exogeneous shocks. Thus, to help narrow the perception gap between the Bank and these groups, it is important for the Bank to enhance its

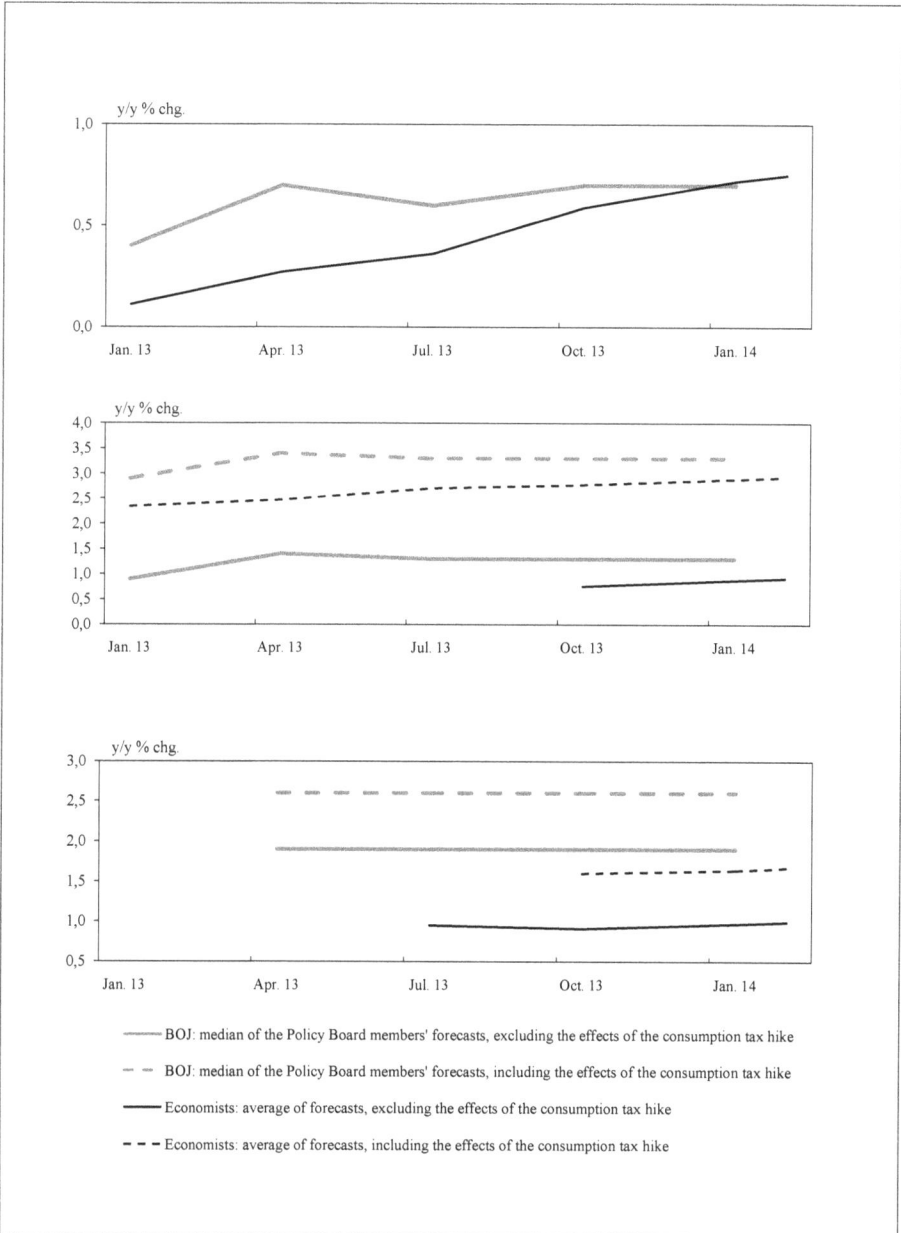

Chart 11

dialogue with them by (1) exchanging views on forecasting methods as well as (2) providing clearer explanations about the transmission mechanism of monetary easing (including background analysis) and the direction of QQE for achieving the target.

Communication to Enhance Public Understanding on the Importance of the 2 Percent Target

The Bank needs to increase its dialogue with the public to promote understanding of the importance of the 2 percent target. In January 2013, the Bank judged that setting the 2 percent price stability target was important for the economy. This judgment took into account, for example, (1) the scope needed to avoid another deflationary period, (2) the scope needed for the conduct of flexible monetary policy in normal periods to avoid the zero lower bound in the recessionary phase of the economy, (3) the upward bias in the CPI statistics, and (4) the need to align with the global standard of a price stability target. Moreover, achieving sufficiently high nominal GDP growth rates is essential for the economy to boost firms' and households' economic growth expectations.

In Japan, the majority of households continue to view price rises as *unfavorable*. This implies that the importance of achieving the 2 percent target may not be widely understood and shared by households. Thus, it is vitally important for the Bank to clearly explain to the public and respond to questions as to why the Bank aims to achieve the 2 percent price stability target and how this will improve daily lives in the medium to long term. This is particularly important given that a consumption tax hike is scheduled in April this year, and the inflation rate may temporarily exceed 2 percent, together with the effects of monetary easing.

Communication about the 2 Percent Pinpoint Target

Some argue that the Bank should adopt an *inflation target range*, rather than an *inflation target point*. I believe that the Bank should maintain the current inflation target point (that is, 2 percent). The idea of applying a *range* to the inflation target should not be ruled out and might be examined after the actual inflation rate exceeds at least 1 percent in a stable manner and after it is judged that inflation expectations are likely to rise toward 2 percent. However, the premature introduction of a range may result in the actual inflation rate getting stuck at the *lower* bound of the range, making it harder to achieve the 2 percent target. A more important concern in this case is that the markets and the public may mistakenly assume that the Bank's intention to achieve the target has weakened, undermining the credibility of monetary policy.

Communication on Achieving the 2 Percent Target in a Stable Manner

Lastly, the expression "in a stable manner" contained in the second description of the Bank's forward guidance may give the impression of ambiguity in terms of its description of the conditions. This expression, however, appears to be appropriate at present, because the formation of long-term inflation expectations entails uncertainty. In addition, judgment on how and when long-term inflation expectations will be stabilized at around 2 percent is likely to require a clear understanding of the features and movements of a range of indicators measuring inflation expectations. Nevertheless, as economic activity and prices firmly improve and as the process of increasing inflation expectations becomes clearer with an enhanced understanding of their developments, I think that the second description of forward guidance could be refined with more specific information about what constitutes "in a stable manner" from a longer-term perspective.

I would like to end my presentation here. Thank you for your kind attention.

2014 US Monetary Policy Forum Participants

1.	William Abecassis	Blackrock Advisors
2.	John Abraham	Morgan Stanley
3.	Lewis Alexander	Nomura Securities
4.	Zahir Antia	Canadian Consulate General
5.	Binyamin Appelbaum	The New York Times
6.	Leslie Barbi	Guardian Life Insurance Co of America
7.	Marvin Barth	Barclays
8.	Karim Basta	III Associates
9.	Joe Beaulieu	Brevan Howard
10.	Steven Beckner	Market News International
11.	Richard Berner	U.S. Department of the Treasury
12.	Ashok Kumar Bhatia	Balyasny Asset Management
13.	Andreas Billmeier	Ziff Brothers Investments
14.	Hayley Boesky	Bank of America Merrill Lynch
15.	Antulio Bomfim	Macroeconomic Advisers, LLC
16.	Beth Ann Bovino	Standard and Poor's Ratings Agency
17.	Christian Broda	Duquesne Family Office
18.	Seamus Brown	Moore Capital
19.	James Bullard	Federal Reserve Bank of Saint Louis
20.	Stephen Cecchetti	Brandeis International Business School
21.	Sun-Byoung Chae	Bank of Korea
22.	Kim Chong	Hong Kong Monetary Authority
23.	James Clark	U.S. Department of the Treasury
24.	Gerald Cohen	The Brookings Institution
25.	Julia Coronado	BNP Paribas
26.	Peter Coy	Bloomberg Businessweek

27.	Anthony Crescenzi	PIMCO
28.	Pedro da Costa	The Wall Street Journal
29.	Troy Davig	Federal Reserve Bank of Kansas City
30.	Steven Davis	University of Chicago
31.	Joseph Deaux	The Street.com
32.	Michael Derby	Dow Jones Newswires
33.	Kenneth deRegt	Canarsie Capital Group
34.	Juhi Dhawan	Wellington Management Company
35.	Michael Dow	UBS Global Asset Management
36.	Sophia Drossos	Element Capital Mangement
37.	James Dutkiewitz	Sentry Investments
38.	Wilson Ervin	Credit Suisse
39.	Marcello Estevao	Tudor Investments Corporation
40.	Charles Evans	Federal Reserve Bank of Chicago
41.	Mark Farrington	Macro Currency Group
42.	John Feldmann	Discovery Capital
43.	Martin Feldstein	NBER
44.	Michael Feroli	JP Morgan Chase
45.	David Fettig	Federal Reserve Bank of Minneapolis
46.	Stanley Fischer	
47.	Robert J. Fitzsimmons	High Road Capital Partners
48.	Ole Frøseth	NBIM
49.	David Gerstenhaber	Argonaut Capital Management
50.	David Greenlaw	Morgan Stanley
51.	Krishna Guha	International Strategy and Investment
52.	Kevin Hall	McClatchy News Service
53.	James Hamilton	University of California, San Diego
54.	Michael Hanson	BofA Merrill Lynch
55.	Robin Harding	Financial Times
56.	Kevin Harrington	Thiel Macro LLC
57.	Ethan Harris	Bank of America Merrill Lynch
58.	Guy P. Haselmann, CAIA	Capital Markets Strategist
59.	Jan Hatzius	Goldman, Sachs & Co.
60.	Deborah Hilibrand	The Hilibrand Foundation
61.	Lawrence Hilibrand	Hilibrand Foundation
62.	Peter Hooper	Deutsche Bank Securities Inc.
63.	Tomoyuki Imachi	Jiji Press New York bureau
64.	Greg Ip	The Economist
65.	Raymond Joseph Iwanowski	SECOR Asset Management
66.	Mo Ji	Azentus Capital Management

67.	Larry Kantor	Barclays Capital
68.	Anil Kashyap	University of Chicago
69.	Takeshi Kato	Bank of Japan, US
70.	Narayana Kocherlakota	Federal Reserve Bank of Minneapolis
71.	Teeraya Krongkaew	Bank of Thailand
72.	Jason Lange	Thomson Reuters
73.	Don Lee	Los Angeles Times
74.	Alan Levenson	T. Rowe Price Associates
75.	Richard Leventhal	Fedway Associates
76.	Alexander Levy	New York University
77.	Nellie Liang	Board of Governors of the Federal Reserve System
78.	Steve Liesman	CNBC
79.	Lorie Logan	Federal Reserve Bank of New York
80.	Gerald Lucas	Brevan Howard
81.	Stephen Lucas	Goldman Sachs
82.	Matthew Luzzetti	Deutsche Bank
83.	Gerard MacDonell	SAC Capital
84.	Dean Maki	Barclays Capital
85.	John Makin	American Enterprise Institute
86.	Gail MarksJarvis	Chicago Tribune
87.	Marco Martella	Banca d'Italia
88.	David Maurice	Barclays
89.	James McAndrews	Federal Reserve Bank of New York
90.	Brian McCarthy	Emerging Sovereign Group
91.	Michael McKee	Bloomberg Television
92.	Loretta J. Mester	Federal Reserve Bank of Philadelphia
93.	Michelle Meyer	Bank of America Merrill Lynch
94.	Margo Miller	Fannie Mae
95.	Frederic Mishkin	Columbia University
96.	Felix Momsen	Govt of Singapore Investment Corp
97.	Patricia Mosser	U.S. Department of Treasury
98.	Fredric A. Nelson III	Commonfund Asset Management Company
99.	Hiroyuki Nishimura	The Nikkei
100.	Vinay Pande	Brevan Howard US Investment Management LP
101.	Zach Pandl	Columbia Management
102.	Gregory Pierce	HSBC
103.	Charles Plosser	Federal Reserve Bank of Philadelphia
104.	Jerome H. Powell	Board of Governors of the Federal Reserve System
105.	Sangeetha Ramaswamy	Herman Global, LLC
106.	John Rivera	Autonomy Capital

107.	David Rogal	BlackRock
108.	Jeff Rosenberg	Blackrock Advisors
109.	Eric Rosengren	Federal Reserve Bank of Boston
110.	Robert E. Rubin	Council on Foreign Relations
111.	Brian Sack	The D.E. Shaw Group
112.	Paul Saltzman	The Clearing House Association
113.	Maurice Samuels	Convexity Capital
114.	George U. Sauter	
115.	Kermit Schoenholtz	NYU Stern School of Business
116.	Jeffrey R. Shafer	JRShafer Insight
117.	Paul Sheard	Standard and Poor's Ratings Agency
118.	Hyun Shin	Princeton University
119.	Sayuri Shirai	Bank of Japan
120.	Torsten Slok	Deutsche Bank
121.	Seamus Smyth	Caxton Associates
122.	Robert Spector	MFS Investment Management Canada
123.	Jes Staley	BlueMountain Capital Management LLC
124.	Sven Jari Stehn	Goldman Sachs
125.	Eric Stein	Eaton Vance
126.	Jeremy C. Stein	Board of Governors of the Federal Reserve System
127.	Amir Sufi	University of Chicago
128.	Daniel G. Sullivan	Federal Reserve Bank of Chicago
129.	Michael Tangney	Colgate-Palmolive Company
130.	Daniel Tenengauzer	Standard Chartered Bank
131.	Gillian Tett	Financial Times
132.	Christopher Thompson	Reserve Bank of Australia
133.	Olivier Luis Trouveroy	MTN Capital Partners
134.	Byron G. Tucker	Nautilus Capital Management Co
135.	Angel Ubide	D.E. Shaw & Co.
136.	Mark Van Wyk	Goldman Sachs Asset Management
137.	Sanjay Verma	Blenheim Capital Management
138.	Ken Volpert	Vanguard
139.	Dane Vrabac	Morgan Stanley
140.	Christopher J. Waller	Federal Reserve Bank of Saint Louis
141.	Jerry Webman	Oppenheimer Funds
142.	John A. Weinberg	Federal Reserve Bank of Richmond
143.	David Wessel	Brookings Institution
144.	Kenneth West	University of Wisconsin
145.	David Wilcox	Board of Governors of the Federal Reserve System
146.	Marcella Williams	

147.	Marilyn Wimp	Federal Reserve Bank of Philadelphia
148.	Martin Wolf	Financial Times
149.	Yuji Yokobori	Bank of Japan
150.	Jeffrey Young	Woodbine Capital
151.	Barry L. Zubrow	ITB LLC
152.	Joshua Zumbrun	Bloomberg News

Acknowledgements

The 2014 U.S. Monetary Policy Forum acknowledges the generous financial support from Kenneth and Anne Griffin. We also wish to thank Michael Feroli and JP Morgan Chase for providing their support for the preparation of the report.

In addition to institutional support, there were a number of people whose help was essential to our success. First, there are all of the members of the USMPF panel, who offered comments and encouragement. Second, we thank the FOMC members, who attended the meeting and spoke on the record. We extend a special thanks to Jerome Powell, Board of Governors of the Federal Reserve System and James Bullard and Eric Rosengren, the Presidents of the Federal Reserve Banks of Saint Louis and Boston, respectively, who accepted our invitation to attend the meeting and participated as members of the audience. Finally, there were several people behind the scenes who deserve special mention. These include Peggy Eppink, Susan Guibert, Sarah Niemann, and Erika Morey of the University of Chicago Booth School of Business. Finally, we owe a special thanks to Jennifer Williams for organizing the conference and overseeing all the conference operations.

www.ingramcontent.com/pod-product-compliance
Lightning Source LLC
Chambersburg PA
CBHW061333220326
41599CB00026B/5170